TABLE OF CONTENTS

Almost Nothing

Almost Nothing

*"My biggest fear is dying alone,
a nobody, with nothing."*

Raheem Akmadir-Nahsif

Dedicated to Shirley Dawson

The only woman I've ever known to give from her heart with no expectations of anything in return, even when the recipients of her selfless kindness were ungrateful, haughty, and undeserving.

The only woman I've ever known to exude superhuman strength and resilience under the most volatile and unrelenting situations.

The only woman I've ever known to endure and overcome formidable adversity: poverty, alcoholism, heartbreak, and betrayal; always with a humble heart and a smile on her beautiful face, humming her favorite song, *"Never Would Have Made It."*

The only woman I've ever known who knew exactly when to give me tough love when I needed it yet was always my biggest cheerleader.

The only woman who loved me even at my worst and even when I didn't see it, she saw the best in me.

The only woman I ever loved unconditionally, sincerely and wholeheartedly.

The only woman I've ever known whose love was like no other love in the world and will reside in the depths of my soul until my last breath...... My Momma.

Acknowledgements

I want to thank Gloria Parker, my rock, my motivator, and most-cherished, dearest friend. The person who has always believed in me and my abilities even when I did not believe in them myself. The person who has supported me and cheered me on when I was going through the most difficult times in my life; always keeping a front row seat in applauding my accomplishments. The person who single-handedly restored my faith in people. The person who taught me that I could heal from my brokenness, who taught me how to love and be loved. I thank you, G. with every bit of who I am.

I'd like to thank Richard Brown, courageous holder of all my secrets and keeper of the details of my greatest fears. He is more than just an N.A. Sponsor. He held me up and supported me at some of my most trying times with no reservations or conditions. He has been the most nurturing source of my recovery; the most trusted sponsor, brother, friend, and father figure anyone could ever pray for. I love him as much as a man can love another man. I stay checking in with Richard so that I don't check out.

I want to thank Kim Rakosky, the editor of this work. She's proven to be not only a fantastic editor but also a supportive and loving friend. She has encouraged me to tell my truth in all its glory or gloom, yet to stay mindful of how its expression comes across to the reader. She has helped me grow as an author and a person. Words are too weak to express my appreciation and gratitude to have her in my life.

I want to thank my son Ibn-Raheem Akmadir-Nahsif, for his birth being the ultimate event that helped me save me from me. His existence makes me mindful that there is a greater responsibility that I must fulfill. He is a constant reminder that I must be an example of the man that I want him to be. His existence reminds me that I must be resilient in all my endeavors; to show him that   no matter what happens in life he must always:

"Stay Grinding', Stay Focused"

I want to thank my beautiful daughter, Irvina Renea (Mama) Gee, for being the light of my life. For being the one person that made me weak with love when I wanted to be strong. For being a Daddy's Girl. For her energetic personality, infectious laughter, and giving heart that makes me love her even more with each thought of her. My heart breaks that she is no longer here in physical form for us to celebrate each other's accomplishments and milestones, but I know somehow, she sees me and is proud of me.

I want to thank my Dad, Leroy Oliver, for demonstrating for me what a humble, strong man is supposed to be. Although he struggled with finances, he was rich with integrity, humility and respect. He taught me how to walk with my head held high no matter what circumstances I went through. He taught me how to be a man amongst men.

I want to thank Steve Johnson who held up the mirror for me to take a clear look at who I was so that I could determine who I wanted to become. He planted the seed, ignited the spark, and fanned the flame of recovery for me. Without his hysterically funny, yet profound, delivery of information; I don't know if I could have imagined the turning point in my life. I will never forget you.

I want to thank Narcotics Anonymous for giving me a message of hope and promising me freedom from active addiction. For proving to me that an addict, any addict, can stop using drugs, lose the desire to use drugs and find a "new way to live." As long as I follow this way, I have nothing to fear.

I want to especially thank my thousands of loyal followers on social media: Instagram, YouTube, TikTok, and Facebook. @AlmostEverything630 and @Raheem Akmadir-Nahsif. They have inspired me to maintain my positive attitude so that I can continue each day to motivate, push and encourage them to always:

"Stay Grindin', Stay Focused."

Finally, I want to thank the various people who I witnessed allowing their evident talents and abilities to wither and die. They may have never known that I was observing or being influenced by their surrender. In that sad scenario they showed me the darkness and shame of unexplored potential and a dream deferred.

Foreword
By KimiGee982

In 2022, I found myself in the midst of a grief-induced, heavy depression, the result of a sudden series of personal losses and a near-death health crisis a few years prior. I was trying different ways to heal my broken heart and restore my joy and usual optimism. A much younger friend of mine introduced me to TikTok, which I had dismissed as a "kid thing." I discovered it was much more than a kid thing. I was pleasantly surprised to find loads of helpful, healing content there. I typed in the word "motivation" and up popped *AlmostEverything630*.

Raheem was talking about the ultimate importance of mindset in relation to changing one's life. This philosophy, and his signature admonition to always *"Stay Grindin', Stay Focused,"* resonated strongly with me. I began following Raheem regularly for motivational pep talks; but I became captivated and intrigued by his powerful, redemptive life journey and his amazing storytelling superpowers.

One of my deep personal losses was the overdose death of my 30-something nephew. He lost his life in an on-again off-again battle with drugs and incarceration. Over the years I had mentored him and tried to guide him as he struggled. As I listened to Raheem's advice and testimony about overcoming self-destruction, I realized that this kind of talk and guidance was exactly what my nephew had needed. As much as I had tried, Auntie was just not equipped with the experience, nor familiar enough with the depth of his pain to be of any substantial help.

As an elementary school teacher in Philadelphia for 22 years, I had experienced children coming to school from all kinds of heartbreakingly traumatic backgrounds. Children mired in trauma also drag it to school and act out in all kinds of disruptive ways. I had a knack for getting through to the most troubled kids, and a determination to try everything to help them achieve success. So, they loaded me up.

I'm sure I learned more from my students than they learned from me. Many reality lessons about the strife and loneliness of growing up and surviving in severely dysfunctional homes. Mostly, I learned about the incredible resilience of children. Children who should be allowed to be children: to grow, learn, play and thrive in safety and love.

Children like Raheem; whose spirits were nearly exterminated, but somehow managed to hang on to find hope and purpose. I thank my now lifetime friend for all his wisdom, and for courageously sharing his often brutal life, all for a greater purpose.

When I learned that Raheem was writing a book, I offered to be his editor. I had worked my way through college by editing scholarly books at Temple University Press. I am deeply honored that he has allowed me to work with him on this project. Publishing this story has been one of Raheem's lifetime dreams.

Some may say Raheem has had a one in a million experience in overcoming his demons and building a meaningful life. His utmost mission, however, extends far beyond mere self-preservation. It is to help others circumstances and to inspire them to take actions to get back in control of their lives.

And for that, Raheem is definitely one in a million in my book!

CHAPTER 1

When the pain gets great

T he smell of urine, defecation and decaying mice filled the air of the small, dilapidated apartment in the building of 408 Monroe Street which the crackheads fondly called "The House That Jack Built." This apartment was in the back of the second floor, right above the rotting garbage in the backyard. I sat down on a cobweb-covered milk crate, disturbing the feces dinner of a rat the size of my size 13 shoes that lay next to it. It shot across the room, straight through a pile of assorted empty bottles and cans before descending upon what appeared to be a fresher pile of feces. Dope fiends, winos, crackheads and bums use these apartments not only to consume their drugs but also to relieve themselves and even sleep.

But on this day, September 10, 1989, I was happy to be there alone. Usually there would be a crowd in each room, either using, begging or trading sex for drugs. There was no one there today to interrupt my daily installment of self-destruction. The sound of the flame from my lighter burning the small rock of crack was like music to my ears. My lips were pressed tightly around the mouthpiece of the homemade pipe and my eyes watched the flame intensely, making absolutely sure I applied just the right amount of heat to the rock of crack so that it burned slowly. It was my last piece. I inhaled the sweet-smelling smoke to the extent my lungs would allow. I held it in for about five seconds, and exhaled, slowly. I didn't know why but I expected another rush, however, that was impossible because I was already as high as anyone could possibly be on crack without going into cardiac arrest.

I had been smoking crack since 2 p.m. the day before. I had stolen all of my girlfriend's food stamps and traded the $473 worth of stamps for $300 cash at the Puerto Rican corner store. It was now 8 pm. I was sweating profusely; my heart was beating a thousand beats per second and my eyes were as wide as two cue balls.

Realizing I had just smoked my last piece of crack. I immediately became anxious and paranoid, looking around on the floor like a desperate rat hoping to recover a rock that I may have unknowingly dropped. But even in my hysterical heart of hearts I knew that a crackhead of my caliber never ever dropped even a crumb. With that in mind, I gathered myself together enough to comprehend that there just was not any more crack and that I would have to go out and get more money from somewhere to get more. I tiptoed to the door (paranoid), opened it, looked around quickly, then walked briskly into the night.

It was Friday and the streets were lively, a day that seemed to put urgency in people's steps. So, aside from my filthy clothes, unshaven face and uncombed hair, the turbo boost the crack had put in my steps probably went unnoticed. Whether folks noticed or not mattered a damn to me at that point. I was now just a few blocks away from my destination and the only thing that mattered to me was crack. I stood in the alley across the street from the Polish Tavern on Hope Avenue waiting for an unsuspecting drunk to exit the bar so that I could "handle my business" and get back to my spot at the House that Jack Built before it got too crowded.

I seemed to have been waiting for hours but had only been waiting a few minutes. My high was fading, and desperation had begun to set in. Consciously, I began taking an inventory of myself. There I stood, I thought, in the darkness of that alley, a shell of a man. A 22-yearold, 6'3", 133-pound crackhead with no real goal in life except to rob, steal, manipulate and take whatever I could get my hands on. I felt that my dignity was nonexistent. I had no self-respect, no self-esteem, no morals, and did not even have clean underwear on. I felt that my life was just a mess.

The sound of footsteps interrupted my thoughts. When I looked in the direction from which they came, there wobbled my victim. A short pudgy man staggered closer to me, unaware of me and my ill intent hiding in darkness of the alley. The man whistled a tune as he walked, snapping his fingers in an attempt at rhythm.

As soon as the man was close enough, I leaped from the darkness and grabbed him around the neck in a chokehold. I did not know if the man reacted impetuously, out of fear, or simply out of his expertise in jujitsu. Before I could utter my infamous stick-up words: "Give it up or I'll kill you," the man had flipped me so fast and so hard onto the ground that my bowels exploded.

The air was knocked clear from my chest. I could not move or talk. I just laid there confused, surprised and shitty. The man immediately dove on top of me and yelled "Someone call de polize for dis son-na-me beetch!!" while he punched my face and head repeatedly.

At that point, I wanted to call the "polize" myself. I could feel my eyes swelling, my nose bleeding and taste the blood in my mouth. "I wish the police would hurry the fuck up," I thought as I struggled to ward off the man's constant flow of punches. The little Polish man had managed to get each of my arms under each of his knees and proceeded to slap me instead of punching me. With each jarring slap, the man added insult: Whopp, You Blaaack beetch!!" Whopp! "Motherfucka beetch!!"

When the police finally arrived and were told what took place, they laughed hysterically and called me every idiot they could think of. In fact, at the police station one of the police officers placed a handwritten sign on the holding cell entry which read: "The Idiot Beetch!"

CHAPTER 2

Character is shaped by experience

As I sat in the holding cell, I began to wonder how I had gotten myself into such messes, figuratively and literally. I guessed the reasons lay in my experiences. I sat there in the cell going over my life. My family was dirt poor growing up. My mother, three sisters and I lived in a two-bedroom apartment in the heart of the chaotic and very dangerous Third Street. The part of Passaic New Jersey where even the police were afraid to go. My father was nonexistent for the most part and there was never really any guidance in my life. I usually did what I wanted to do whenever I wanted to do it, because my Mom was usually either passed out, too drunk to realize the things I was doing, or she was too busy trying to navigate the mess of her own life.

I didn't want to be me. I hated me. I hated how I looked and how I was living. I hated the horrors I faced each night, being raped by a female family "friend"; and I hated where I lived. I hated that I didn't I have all the things I thought I should have for a child to thrive; and I hated how my life's situation made me feel all the time. I hated feeling sad, or lonely, or angry, scared, frustrated, ugly, confused, hungry, inadequate, ashamed and thinking that I would die before I reached 18 years old. I hated it, and I wanted to be someone else.

I hung out with older boys when I was younger because, not only did they give me the elixir (weed and beer) to forget my reality and dull my emotions, they also supplied me with a feeling of importance and a sense of belonging. The boys my age would always make fun of how old and dirty my clothes were, how buck my teeth were, and how pork fat (fatback) and grits were the only things my family could afford to eat. The older boys didn't really care about what I looked like or what I ate. Their only concern was how well I could steal and how poorly I fought at that time. Because how well I fought determined my share of the things I stole. And considering how small I was compared to the older boys I almost always was left with little or nothing of what I stole. Still, I hung out with them because I felt like I belonged with them, like I was a part of something that not only needed me but also wanted me. That was all I cared about.

By the time I was nine years old I could run inside a clothing store, scoop up an armful of sweaters and be gone before security ever knew what hit them. By 10, I could snatch a woman's purse or rip an old man's wallet from his pocket so fast that the only description they would have been able to give the police was: "the back of his head was nappy, and the bottom of his shoes had holes in them," because that would have been the only thing they had seen.

By the time I had reached 11 years old I was thoroughly respected by the older guys, because not only did I make the most money, but I was also the most dangerous. And although I still could not fight very well, I was notorious for picking up whatever I could get my hands on to equalize the fighting field. I then began to receive an almost equal share of most of the things I stole.

Being 11 was a very confusing time for me. Besides coming to grips with, and somewhat understanding of my mother's alcoholism, I also began to think and comprehend differently. Things didn't seem to be as simple and meaningless to me as they had been.

I remember going to the neighborhood grocery store called Big John's as a child to buy myself a pack of Now and Later candy. While standing in line to be waited on, a mother who had also been waiting in line in front of me with her young son began stroking the boy's head lovingly, then kissed the boy atop his head and said, "I love you," in a way that I suspected only a mother can say. "I love you too Mommy," the boy cooed.

As I walked out of the store on my way back home, I couldn't help wondering why my Mom had never said those words to me. I knew my mother loved us, in her own way, because we were her children. But at that point, I had never heard my Mom or anyone else speak those words to me. I didn't fully understand the real magnitude of love at that age. But what I did understand is that when someone said they love you, it meant that they cared about what happens to you.

I never doubted my Mom's love for her family. In fact, I knew she loved us as best she could, despite her alcoholism. I imagined the intent behind the things she would do for us was out of love. I mean, she fed us, she always yelled at us if we were not in the house at a certain time, and she always kept any appointments and appearances she needed to make on our behalf. Besides, I was learning firsthand how drinking could quickly become a priority. I knew it was imperative that I forget certain aspects of my life to deal with life in general. So, I assumed there were some things my mama needed to forget for herself.

Love, I imagined, was the primary thing for her to forget, because just the mention of my father's name would change the whole mood and the expression on my mother's face. She never really had anything bad to say about him other than he had married a woman who had a prosthetic leg. Well, "one leg Bitch" is how she described the woman. But my Mom would light up and simultaneously become angry at just the mention of Leroy's name. Love, I reasoned, at our house, was a thing somehow understood rather than expressed. Yet, I was confused as to why.

CHAPTER 3

It's not your fault

Actually, "confused" is too weak a word to describe the 11th year of my life. My Mom would hold card game parties, which a lot of the women did in the neighborhood around the first of the month when folks got their welfare checks in order to help pay the bills the checks did not cover. These card games went on well into the early morning hours. My sisters and I would have to spend the night at my Mom's best friend's apartment.

Janet was a very tall and an unusually skinny woman who looked like a horse in the face. Her head was abnormally thin, and her skin was always ashy, which made the huge bumps and open sores on her face look even more horrifying. Her breath stayed smelling like hot garbage and her teeth were a variety of colors, mostly green, yellow, black and Budweiser bottle brown. They were all broken, chipped and very sharp-looking. I imagined that the devil had broken a beer bottle and shoved the shards of glass into her gums to act as teeth. Janet's tongue seemed fat and covered with a thick white coating which made it appear heavy and hard. She wore a dusty grey scarf around her head, and a food-, urine-, and what looked like a blood-stained, flower printed, grayish housecoat every day. I could not remember ever seeing her sober. All the children who lived in the building were absolutely terrified of her. We nicknamed her Broom Hilda. Broom Hilda the Witch. The name fits her like a glove.

Broom Hilda's daughter, Chandra, and I had been watching television in the living room before falling asleep on the couch, when suddenly I was awakened by the loud talking and laughing of a man and woman. I recognized Broom Hilda's voice immediately, but the man's voice sounded like Michael Bryson. However, it couldn't be Michael Bryson, I figured, because it was three in the morning and Michael was only 16 years old. Besides, I thought, what would Michael Bryson be doing at Broom Hilda's house (who was at least 40 years old), in her bedroom, at three in the morning?

The last time I saw Michael Bryson, I remembered, was about a year before. He, a guy named BigHead Bobby, and I were in a construction site trailer we called a clubhouse smoking cigarettes and weed. Michael ordered me to go out to find the neighborhood lady wino called Cat Food and tell her that Michael wanted to fuck her. I laughed, thinking Michael was joking, until I saw the seriousness in his eyes and heard the urgency in his voice as he repeated, "Tell her I said I want to fuck her," Michael ordered angrily. I was confused a little, but I suspected that Cat Food wasn't who he really wanted to fuck. I wandered around town not really looking for Cat Food, but had I run into her I would have told her what Michael Bryson said, just for kicks.

When I returned 30 minutes later, unsuccessful at my half-hearted attempt to locate Cat Food, I found Michael wiping off his huge penis and a crying BigHead

Bobby pulling up his pants. When I asked BigHead why he was crying, he looked at Michael, whose face had taken on an evil stare. BigHead Bobby then answered, "I was beaten ma meat, and it hurt when I came." "Aun hunh," I replied, spun right back around and ran straight back out of the door, thinking, "Lawd Ham Mercy!" I ran far, far away from Michael Bryson.

Things had gotten quiet, and I wondered what was going on. I got off the couch, onto my knees and crawled near the kitchen door. No one was there. As I crawled through the kitchen towards the bedroom, I began to hear Broom Hilda asking God to help her. "Oh, Gawd hep me, hep me please, this thang good. Ooooooh Lawd hep me," she cooed. When I reached the bedroom door there he was, Michael Bryson was in between Broom Hilda's legs slamming himself against her like a freight train. With each thrust his body pushed Broom Hilda's head closer and closer to the headboard. Within seconds her head was hitting the headboard so hard I expected her head to be a bloody mess. But no matter how hard he slammed against her she didn't seem to care about a possible head injury, she just continued telling the "Lawd" how good that "thang" was to her. After what seemed like hours of brutal battle, Michael lifted himself from atop her and began walking towards the kitchen.

I quickly crawled to the back of the kitchen, out of sight, and watched Michael gather his clothes from a kitchen chair. He walked towards the door with his clothes across his arms as if he was about to walk out the door in his underwear, but as soon as he opened the door, in walked another guy who I later found out was named Darryl Newsom. They both laughed quietly, gave each other dap, and as Michael put on his clothes Darryl pulled his off. Michael left, and Darryl walked slowly into Broom Hilda's bedroom.

When I was sure Michael was gone and imagined that Darryl was "doing it" to Broom Hilda, I crawled near the bedroom door and looked in. Darryl wasn't slamming his body against Broom Hilda's as hard as Michael had. Broom Hilda wasn't talking to God either. Darryl just moved his body against Broom Hilda's in a slow circular motion, kind of like slow dancing, I thought. Instead of yelling at God, Broom Hilda just made noises as if her stomach was hurting: "ooooh, yessssss, ahhhhhh." Broom Hilda moaned until Darryl's body shook like he was having a seizure. Shortly after, he too, gathered his clothes and headed out the door.

I waited for a while, and then came out from behind the stove to lock the door. It was then about five in the morning, and I was hungry after watching all that grown-up stuff. I had talked about "getting some pussy" when the fellas and I sat around talking trash but had never actually done it. I suspected, after witnessing what I just witnessed, none of the other guys had either. The only guys in the crew who may have really "gotten some pussy" might have been Eddie Townsend and Barry McDaniel, I reasoned. Girls loved them because they were the coolest of the clique. I was not exactly sure what made them the coolest, because the both of them had bowlegs and were short, I thought. However, whatever it was, they had it, and the girls loved it.

After eating up all of Broom Hilda's Spam and her last four slices of bread, I stood at the kitchen sink getting a glass of water when Broom Hilda staggered from the bedroom into the kitchen, butt naked. Her tall bony body looked like a skeleton covered with skin. She walked hunched over, swaying from side to side trying to straighten the scarf atop her head as she did. The sight of her flat, little ashened butt cheeks as she passed me, brought the taste of the Spam sandwich back into my mouth. As soon as she stepped into the bathroom, I shot out of the apartment like a bat out of hell.

I ran down to my family's apartment and found that the door was slightly open and saw that my mother was passed out at the table. I immediately looked for the box my mother kept the cut money in, which was a percentage of money collected from every hand played. I looked everywhere I could think of but could not find it anywhere. Everyone had gone home, so I imagined that my mother had hidden the money before she passed out, or perhaps one of her guests took it before I got a chance to steal a few dollars.

I decided to go to bed and fell asleep almost immediately. I was awakened about an hour later by my nightly piss. It never failed; no matter how hard I tried to wake up to go to the bathroom I could never do it. I always pissed in the bed. I tried everything from using the bathroom just before I went to bed to even sleeping in the bathroom, but nothing ever worked. I always woke up wet and pissy. However, I noticed that when I slept over at a friend's house or a relative's house, I would be okay, I rarely pissed in their bed. But as soon as I got in my own bed, I would piss in no time flat.

I took the soiled sheets off the bed and threw them into a plastic garbage bag along with my underwear. I went into the bathroom and stood near the sink with my t-shirt and a piece of soap to wash myself off so that I could jump back onto the same pissy mattress in the same pissy spot to go back to sleep. I stood there washing myself while watching myself in the mirror, paying special attention to my genital area. I toyed around there with the warm soapy t-shirt until my penis was completely erect. I stood there looking at it through the mirror, wondering if every 11-year-old boy's penis grew to such length when it was erect. I had seen other boy's penises when we would put on our shorts for gym class in the locker room at school, and when my friends and I would take pisses outside. I didn't notice any difference in my penis from the other boys, but when my penis got erect, it looked abnormally long and thick for a boy my age, I thought.

Suddenly, the door flew open, hitting the wall with a thunderous BOOM, and Broom Hilda fell through the entrance to the floor. "Moo out da way boy, I gotta pee," she growled, scrambling to get to the toilet. Broom Hilda sat on the toilet grunting and farting. She stared at me with her piercing bloodshot eyes as I stood there covering myself with both hands and the wet, soapy tshirt that doubled as a washcloth. I was half afraid that she saw what I was doing to myself and half confused as to why she would be barging into our bathroom at this time of morning talking about she gotta pee. Broom Hilda stood up, pulling up her filthy pink panties displaying the wet, brownish, yellowish stained crotch. "Yo Momma got any mo licka round here? I looked everywhere, and I cain't find it nowhere. Where it at?" Broom Hilda questioned, as slobber slid down the corner of her mouth.

Still stunned and unable to think of what to say, I shrugged my shoulders and turned to walk out of the bathroom. But, in mid-step, Broom Hilda grabbed my arm. "What you was doing in here, wit yo bad ass?" she asked mischievously," "Moo yo hands boy!" she ordered, snatching my hands away from my private parts. I tried

14

to pull away from her, but she yanked me back in front of her and smacked my head, hard. "Didn't I say move yo gotdam hands boy?" Broom Hilda yelled, as another cloudy stream of drool slid down her chin. My penis had shriveled up immediately and tears began to flow from my eyes as I reluctantly removed my hands. "Let me see what you got," she said in a throaty voice. She began to caress my genitals with her rough, ashy hands. Repulsed and extremely afraid I began to cry audibly, "Momma .... Momma." Broom Hilda's dirty fingernails dug into my testicles.

"If you don't shut yo fucken mouth!" she barked. I was quiet, but my tears flowed heavily. "What's wrong with you, why yo thang won't get up?" Broom Hilda asked, obviously irritated.

Broom Hilda slid down on her knees and took my entire penis into her mouth. I was trembling with fear, thinking that she would bite it or swallow it, and the doctors would have to operate on her to remove my testicle and penis from her stomach. I nearly fainted, grasping for something to hold onto so that I didn't hit the floor. "Momma," I whimpered. Back up on her feet, looking frustrated, she snatched me by the hand and led me to the bedroom and practically threw me onto the bed. "And if you make an-bit of sound I'ma whip yo muthafucken ass," she whispered in an irritated tone. Broom Hilda positioned herself in between my legs and picked up where she left off in the bathroom. She sucked, kissed and licked my genitals as I lay there with my eyes shut tightly, crying and wondering why she was doing this to me. She grabbed the base of my penis and began bobbing her head up and down slowly, moaning like she was sucking on a chicken bone with gravy on it. She made slurping noises and wet licking sounds.

As scared and confused as I was, I began to gradually become erect. I was baffled. None of this felt good to me. I was not enjoying this. My childish mind was racing a mile a minute. Once fully erect, Broom Hilda pushed my legs together and straddled me. I opened my eyes slightly to see what she was doing. Broom Hilda grinned a shit-eating grin, pulled her smelly housecoat over her head to take it off, slid her filthy panties to the side and reached down between them to take hold of my penis. She shoved it into her, grunted and began to thrust her lower body hard against my stomach, hurting me. It felt like I was being punched in the stomach, I thought.

Broom Hilda began to move her head from side to side as a thick, cloudy stream of saliva slid down her chin. I closed my eyes again tightly and pretended I was somewhere else when suddenly she grabbed me by the back of the head, and in one swoop, had my head pressed tightly against her small, shriveled breast. Broom Hilda began to breathe heavily. Her breath reeked of alcohol and what smelled like hot shit. She pounded herself against me harder and harder until her frail body began to shudder uncontrollably. She sank her long, sharp, dirty fingernails into my shoulders until I squealed in pain. Then, she pulled my head upward with both hands. Slobber oozed from her mouth, down her chin and onto my face as she cooed, "I love you; I love……you, I……. love ……yooou."

Before leaving, Broom Hilda put a crumbled dollar bill in my hand and sternly warned, "If you tell yo Momma I will get that extension cord and tear yo ass up, you hear me?!!" I was confused and still shaking, nodding yes, as Broom Hilda swayed through the door to leave. I jumped up, ran in the bathroom, practically dove into the dirty bathtub and turned on the water. I positioned my genitals right under the faucet and washed myself vigorously as the water flowed. I desperately wanted the smell and feel of Broom Hilda off me. All I could think of was her voice saying: "I love you, I love......you, I.......... love.......yooou." I shook my head violently to shake the words out of my head, but they played in my head over and over again. I wanted to tell my mother what happened, but I felt that since I was always getting into trouble and lying so much, she would never believe me. I figured it best to keep that nightmare to myself.

Nearly every night thereafter Broom Hilda would find her way into my room, molesting me, raping me, and threatened to kill me if I ever said anything to anybody about what she was doing to me. I felt trapped. Like I was stuck in a horrible nightmare. And I did not believe anyone cared that I was stuck there. I felt alone, scared and hopeless. I felt like nothing.

One night I heard the front door to our apartment squeak open. Before I knew it, the very tall and abnormally skinny Broom Hilda stood in the dark entrance to my room, swaying from side to side, apparently drunker than usual. I pretended to be asleep, hoping that she would turn and wobble away, but experience had shown me that it was at those times when she was even more vile, brutal and unrelenting. She crept toward my bed like a lioness stalking a calf. I could hear my heart beating hard against my chest, and I could almost smell her sour breath emitting a disgusting odor from her mouth, see her brown, yellow/greenish, broken, sharp mangled teeth, and feel her thick, hard, white mucus-covered tongue trying to force its way into my mouth. "Mama," I began to whimper, "Mama, please help me, Mama." "Shut yo mouth, you little black muthafucka!" Broom Hilda ordered.

When I peeked through my eyelids, I could see Broom Hilda reach in between her legs and pull out a bloody, heavy-looking, miniature pillow. The smell that followed was so pungent and foul that I got an instant headache, my eyes began to burn, and I could taste the vomit coming from my stomach. She slung the bloody mess against the wall, simultaneously wrapped her skinny fingers around my throat, dug her dirty nails into my skin, and straddled my face. "Mama," I tried to yell, but the pressure of Broom Hilda's hand around my throat, the suffocating funky smell from her vagina, and the thick clots of blood that filled my mouth left me voiceless.

After what seemed like hours of sliding and smearing funk and blood all over my face and head, her body began to convulse uncontrollably as she grinded her crotch against my mouth and nose harder and faster. She held on tighter and tighter to my head, sinking her sharp nails into my skull. "Yes, yes!" she moaned. Gradually, her hard, quick thrust became slow, methodical, back and forth motions. "Yes, you little muthafucka," she whispered. "I love you. I love you so fucken much," as she collapsed on my head.

Finally, rolling over onto her side, she grabbed hold of my bloody, skinny, and stinking face to turn it toward her. "Look at me," she spat between clenched teeth, "You ain't shit. You ain't never gone be shit. You better hope that big black funky dick of yours stay workin'. 'Cause if it evvver stop workin' ain't nan Bitch in the world gone want yo ugly ass. Plus, you black, dumb and you sneaky. You ain't shit. You almost nothing."

Even at that tender age, I knew that this traumatic event would confuse my perspective about women, sex, and especially love. But more than anything else, I knew I would spend a lifetime trying to forget everything Broom Hilda had ever said and done to me.

CHAPTER 4

Jamesburg "University"

That morning, coupled with the memories of plenty of other horrid times, caused me to start staying away from home all night to avoid the grips of Broom Hilda.

I couldn't figure out why she did these terrible nasty things to me. I mean, she had grown men to do this shit with. Why me? I thought. What was it about me that made her pursue and degrade me the way she did? What did I do to her? Was I in some way asking for this shit? Was it my behavior? The way I looked? I began to believe that I was in some way responsible for her doing that shit to me. I just did not know how. It physically hurt my brain trying to figure it out.

Eventually, I began to believe what she said about me not being shit. She said I would end up dead before I reached the age of 18. Or, she said, I would end up in prison for the rest of my life. I believed her and therefore had no regard for my life or the quality of it. I began to live the way I believed.

By staying out I got into more trouble and was sent to a juvenile reformatory for snatching an old woman's purse. Jamesburg State Home for Boys and Girls. I was 13 years old, and to me, Jamesburg was not punishment... it was a vacation. I ate three meals a day, had snacks every night at 8 p.m., learned how to play basketball, got medical and dental attention, saw movies three times a week and even found the courage to speak to girls. I silently wished that I could stay there for as long as I wanted to. I was having the time of my life.

However, I did miss my Mom and sisters very much. I even wished that my sisters were there too, so that they could experience some of the joy I was experiencing. Especially the food. Most of the kids there complained about the food, but I loved the fact that I ate so many different things so many times a day, instead of the fatback and grits my sisters and I ate every day. I knew my sisters would enjoy it too.

I often thought about my Mom as well and hoped that she was okay. I never even imagined that she would have stopped drinking, because as long as I could remember she had always drank. Yet, I missed her and loved her dearly. I had even promised myself that I would try harder to take better care of her and my sisters.

The only downside to being in Jamesburg, if there was one, was that there were so many different personalities to manage. I was put in Cottage 10, the cottage where the older, problematic kids were placed. Although I wasn't particularly problematic or as old as the other boys, the nature of my crime suggested that I was. Robbery was considered a violent crime. So, I was placed in the cottage where like-minded kids were. I seemed to realize that every person had their own way of thinking, acting and or behaving, and I found it important to know the personalities of the people I encountered. I felt that the better I knew the person's personality pattern the more equipped I was to deal with their behavior.

If Muquadeen, a tall, dark, bow-legged dude from Newark (who was snaggle-toothed with a violent temper) was in an aggressive mood on a particular day, I knew to either avoid him or talk to him in a way that made him feel like the most feared person in the world. I learned early that a bully always needed to be validated. A bully always needs to have someone else tell him how awesome he is. I imagined those ego boosters either masked his fear and/or fed his stupidity. Either way, I figured he was a coward too dumb to be scared.

Then, there was Brickhouse, a short, stout, younger dude from Jersey City who found pleasure in stirring up drama between people so that he could watch them fight. This dude stayed working out morning, noon, and night. I believed that Brickhouse stirred up shit between people to keep attention away from himself and worked out all the time to put doubt or fear in anybody's mind that might question his fighting ability. I knew to either avoid him or challenge him. In front of everybody.

Jamesburg was not only a fun escape from the dark and arduous life I knew, but it was also a school of sorts. It taught me that people are only as strong as the power you give them to be. If people believed a certain thing about you, they would behave or act in accordance to what they believed about you. No matter if it was true or not. People often lived the way they believed.

The time I spent at Jamesburg was pretty much uneventful. I only really associated with the people from Passaic County. That's pretty much how it was, "you get down with your homies." Passaic County was deep. They had the largest population there. Essex County was the runner up. Then, maybe Camden and Bergen County. I tried to stay low-key and under the radar. However, my buck teeth usually flared up a laugh or two. But I had long ago developed thick skin and could take a joke, as well as tell one.

One evening I was in the dayroom playing a card game called Casino with my homie Nasim.

Nasim was from the Alabama Projects in Paterson. He, even at that young age was a Hood Legend. He was known for liking to smoke Angel Dust, sniffing what he called "Funk Monkey" (Heroin), robbing, and fighting. We took a liking to each other right away. I don't know why I liked this dude. Initially, he used to call me Shitty Mouth. He said my breath was always smelling like shit. But I never could tell, I brushed my tongue and everything.

Anyway, he was funny as hell but took no shorts. Nasim was a fearless dude. He was only about 5'4" tall with a medium build, but he had the heart of a fucken Silver Back Gorilla. It didn't really take much for him to be ready to fight the biggest dude in the cottage. All anyone had to say is: "What you wanna do?" and he would be tying up his sneakers ready for battle, and he won most times.

Brickhouse eased over to the table with another dude named New York. He and New York were from Jersey City, but New York was a young smooth dude. Hustlertype, moneygetting, no drama-type dude. However, like most guys there, he loved a good laugh.

So, when Brickhouse began clowning me about my buck teeth, New York laughed just as hard as everybody else. But when Brickhouse tried to coax New York into hurling his own jokes, New York dug it immediately. "What dat Nigga look like New York?!" Brickhouse asked, bent over in laughter, expecting a joke just as funny. New York replied: "I don't know Nigga, you the comedian," New York chuckled, looking him in the face. "What, you scared of that little Nigga?" He questioned, irritated. "Nah Nigga," New York said indifferently, "I ain't scared of dat Nigga or nan 'nutha Nigga. But you got the jokes tho," he said, half laughing, half seriously. Just as Brickhouse was about to reply, I interrupted: "Come on, big, funny, short, feminine-ass, tight-shirtwearing Nigga. Let's hear another one," I said, smirking. "But first, tie your t-shirt up in a knot in front of you over that big-ass gut, girlfriend." The dayroom exploded in laughter.

"What, muthafucka? I'll whoop yo young ass up in here!!" he spat. Nasim leaned over and whispered: "Fuck dat Nigga up Rah." "Let's go in the mop room, Nigga," I offered calmly, as I stood up and walked toward the mop room, (which was actually a cell in the back of the cottage used to store the brooms, mops, buckets, and cleaning supplies). Mr. Kelly had heard everything. "Close the door behind y'all. And ain't nobody going to the hospital if one of y'all dumb asses gets hurt." He grinned that sinister grin, baring the monogrammed gold tooth he was famous for.

As I walked toward the mop room, I began to wonder how I was gonna get the jump on this humongous dude. I mean, I figured he probably couldn't fight, but he was big as hell and, no doubt, as strong as a country mule. I knew if he got a good hold on me, it would be over. So, I slowed down a bit as we reached the door so that he was just a step or two behind me. I could hear him breathing hard as we got closer to the mop room. The crowd's murmur had me amped. I could feel droplets of sweat slide down my underarm, my heart was beating a mile a minute, and I could feel this surge of energy welling up inside me.

As soon as I walked through the door, I spun around and hit this big Nigga as hard as I could, square on the chin. I don't know if it was the momentum from him walking forward that added to the power of that punch, but his whole body seized up like an old '67 Chevy truck engine. His eyes rolled to the back of his head, and he fell straight back, hitting the ground like a heavy suitcase, flat as day old beer. "Oh shit!!!" the crowd roared in unison. "You see that shit?" "That Nigga out cold!!!" Hysterical laughter filled the room as Brickhouse began to snore.

The crowd began to hurl suggestions; "Do him dirty Nigga, bust him in the head wit one of dem mopwringers," "Piss on that Nigga," "stomp his ass out!" Normally, one or all of these things would happen to a dude if they got knocked out, especially if you didn't want them coming back at you. However, for whatever reason, I let it go at that. New York slapped the Nigga a few times to wake him up, and the same dudes who were yelling for me to do him dirty helped him to his feet and to his cell, probably trying to gas him up to get back at me. Nasim and I finished our card game while watching Brickhouse's cell door to see if he wanted to try it again. He didn't come out until breakfast the next morning. He didn't say anything to me. He just shot rocks (mean stares) at me for the rest of my time there.

CHAPTER 5

Change is inevitable

The nine months I spent in Jamesburg seemed to fly past. Before I knew it, I was back home with my sisters and Mom. Nothing had really changed much except that my older sister Dee Dee was now liking boys rather than beating them up. My middle sister was a little more talkative, my youngest sister just followed the middle sister around, and Mom seemed to be drinking a little more.

Broom Hilda seemed to have found herself a live-in boyfriend whom, I thought, looked like he was always crying. His name was Jeffrey. His eyes were always red and watery, his face was always frowned, and his nose always seemed to be running. He and Broom Hilda were virtually inseparable, yet almost two weeks after I was home, Broom Hilda, grinning like a Cheshire Cat, made her way to my room. "I know yo ass is woke boy," she whispered.

I began to stay away from home again to avoid Broom Hilda and quickly fell back in line with my friends. Nothing with them had changed much except that they were smoking a lot more weed and drinking a whole lot more beer. Which is exactly what I felt I needed. I mean, I had been gone for a significant amount of time, yet nothing had changed. I had begun to figure this was what my life was meant to be: drugs, crime, abuse, and jail. Being high was my only escape.

Of course, we committed more crimes to pay for it, which was fine with me. I had learned a few new tricks or two while in Jamesburg, and I could not wait to show them off. A lot of the guys (especially from Bergen County) talked about B and E (Breaking and Entering) like it was the new way to reach orgasm. They made it seem so easy and lucrative that I couldn't wait to try it. There was an appliance store next to Goodman's Bakery at the corner of Third and Mercer Streets. It was pretty much encased in gates, so the only way in, I thought, was through the roof. I didn't think it out at all. But I told two of my friends, Johnathan and Benjamin, that I had it all mapped out. My plan was to pry up the roof shingles, tear up the tar paper, break through the wood, and be in like Flynn. Never giving any thought as to how we would get the appliances out of the store.

But that was no matter, as soon as my feet hit the floor of the store the alarm sounded. "Oh shit," I said aloud, while trying to stand on top of a refrigerator to get back out of the hole.

"Yo, Ben, Johnny!!" I frantically called. "Yo, where y'all at?!" I yelled. They were long gone. As soon as the alarm sounded, both of them ran like the building was on fire.

"Muthafuckas" I sighed, deflated. I heard the police sirens getting closer and closer. So, I sat atop the fridge and waited.

CHAPTER 6

If nothing changes, nothing changes

Nothing had changed much about Jamesburg. I had only been gone for two months. Most of the people I had left there were still there. Even Brickhouse. Nasim had gone home a week before I got back. My crime was not as bad as the first time, so I was put in Cottage 4. The kids in this cottage were "less confrontational," but my opinion was that we were all the same in kind. They had all heard about my encounter with Brickhouse, so I was kind of given the respect due. However, my buck teeth were still something to laugh about. I didn't mind though. As I said, I could clown dudes with the best of them.

One evening me and a dude from Atlantic City named Al-Basim, a short, light-skinned, chubby dude was sitting in the TV area just chilling, when Mr. Johnson walked in. Mr. Johnson was cool with everybody, except that he was a "by the book" kind of guy. Al-Basim was eating an apple. There was no eating in the TV room. He mentioned the rule to Al-Basim. Mr. Johnson's left arm could not fully extend. I didn't know why, but he always walked around with it half extended. I found it funny. So, to be funny, I spat venomously: "Get the fuck outta here man, let me put a white napkin over that arm Nigga, so you can go wait some tables or something." Al-Basim was huddled over in loud laughter. I saw the anger well up in Mr. Johnson's face immediately. "Either you guys gonna leave out this TV room or I'm gonna write both of you up." "Why you always gotta be acting like that man?" Al-Basim questioned, with a serious, sinister look on his face, while walking toward Mr. Johnson.

I didn't know what the fuck Al-Basim was thinking or why, but I was there. And, it has always been an understood rule that it is always the inmates against the officers. So, before I knew it, myself and about six of the other guys who had overheard the back and forth, had Mr. Johnson surrounded. That look of anger on Mr. Johnson's face turned to fear. "Back up, back the fuck up y'all, I'm warning y'all, back up," he demanded pleadingly. I sensed that he would try to run to the office, so I stood behind him blocking the path.

Mr. Johnson, panicked, began looking around wide-eyed and sweating. "Back up!! Back up!!" Suddenly, Mr. Johnson spun around with that left arm fully extended and punched me square in the mouth with it, knocking my two front teeth down my throat. Horrified, as I lay on the floor choking, Al-Basim had scooped Mr. Johnson up and slammed him on the floor. They all stomped and punched on this dude until the Goon Squad arrived.

After getting our asses whooped, we all ended up in G.U. (Guidance Unit) Lock up, for 60 days. During which time I mourned the loss of my teeth as well as celebrated the loss of them muthafuckas. They had been the bane of my existence for a long time. My only concern was what I look like without them. I went from bucktooth to no teeth, which would probably warrant a whole new series of jokes.

I wasn't too worried about that though. I had been called a bunch of shit before this: pissy, stupid, dirty, ugly, nappy head, and buckteeth were just a few names that I had become impervious to. My self-esteem had taken such a blow that I had developed humor as a coping mechanism, to manage or circumvent the feeling that came with being called all that shit. So, whatever names people came up with to call me probably wouldn't affect me too much more. However, adding one more name to that list was nothing to look forward to.

The entire cottage was split up, we were all sent to different cottages. I was sent to Cottage 12, which was for older dudes, and for the academically inclined. I was neither. I don't know why they decided on sending me to that cottage. I was only 15 and I had been kicked out of school during my 7th grade year; just before the first time at Jamesburg. However, I made the best of it. I found out through taking a GED prep test that I had some academically redeeming qualities.

A professor from Middlesex County College who taught the English class gave us a descriptive writing assignment. Mine was to describe the green footlocker in the dorm that each of the inmates had. I described it in a way in which he thought was above average. He said that he had never witnessed anyone my age and in this incarcerated situation demonstrate such skill. He suggested that I hone my writing skills. He said that I may have significant talent in writing. I felt good about him saying that. I mean, up until that point, there was nothing about myself that I felt good about.

So, I took it and ran with it. I wrote a play for the institution's Talent Show. I managed to get some dudes to perform it on stage, which demonstrated to me that the play must have been good, because none of the dudes that I was associated with would risk being involved with something "corny" or subject themselves to being laughed at. The play received a standing ovation from the inmates as well as the guards and administrative staff.

I even wrote two poems for the institution's Family Day. Both of which received standing ovations as well. I remember the look of pride on my Mama's face as everyone stood and some of my closest associates began chanting my name in approval.

One of the poems was called *I Want to Change*. It referenced the popular clothes we wore at that time (mockneck sweaters and Lee jeans) and hanging out on the block and selling drugs as a method to being seen as opposed to being recognized for any academic, intellectual, or legal entrepreneurial skills we may have had. For the most part, the poem was about change and the fear of it.

I found that writing was certainly a talent I didn't know I had. I even passed the GED prep test, which felt like the biggest thing in the world to me. Because all my young life I had been told that I was stupid and could not achieve anything. Because I had begun to believe that I was stupid, I was overwhelmed by emotion when I learned that I had passed. I remember holding back tears when we were given the results of the test.

I felt accomplished, like I was becoming something good. I was given dentures to replace my missing teeth, which added value to my new view of who I was becoming. My release date was in 10 days. For the first time ever, I felt different. Like I could change.

CHAPTER 7

Experience has always been the best teacher

My Mom had moved Uptown. She lived in a three-story, red brick building on Monroe Street. The building was nestled between a laundromat and a bodega. The big avocado green entrance door to the building was dented, weather beaten, and discolored due to natural wear and tear, and the knocking and kicking on it from the tenants who would often lose or forget their key.

The move from the environment that I was used to was more than just a big change in scenery. I was used to everyone and everything being familiar. Comfortable. However, I quickly realized that although the area and the faces changed, our family situation and the environmental issues remained the same, or worse.

My Mom met new men, new drinking buddies and new places to hang out. My oldest sister Dee Dee started to really feel herself. She began drinking and hanging out with older dudes and staying away from home a lot. Her relationship with my Mom had changed as well. At one time my Mom seemed to rely on Dee to pick up her slack: like watching over us while she was gone and making sure my little sisters ate and were in the house at a certain time. But all that seemed to have changed. She became a whole other person. Smoking, drinking, and hanging out with older men. I was worried about her being in this different environment with these different people. It just appeared to me that the people Uptown were different from Downtown people.

It was weird to me how the area looked better than Third Street, but the goings-on appeared to be 10 times worse. Third Street seemed to be a place where although the mommas drank, the daddies got high, and the brothers and sisters did whatever they did; no matter what, they seemed to stay together. I mean, they fought, and cussed each other out, but at the end of the day, they were still a family. And everybody had everybody's back. Uptown appeared to be a whole 'nutha beast. Like survival of the fittest beast. Family or not.

Coming from Third Street was like wearing a bull's eye on my back. The dudes from this new area recognized a certain difference in my flow and constantly challenged me. I was constantly asked where I was from and who I was related to. When my answers didn't ring any bells, I almost always ended up having to fight or getting jumped. Randy and Chauncy (brothers, originally from Downtown), Don and Gary (who were also brothers), and Marlen were my biggest foes. And they were always together. These dudes fucked with me every chance they got. On the bus, at #11 School Park, Main Avenue, or even in front of my building. It didn't matter where we saw each other. I knew I either had to fight (which ended up with me being jumped) or run. Since I was outnumbered, I figured I'd avoid them until I figured out a way to deal with them.

Avoiding them kept me in or around my building most days, so I got to know the people who lived in the building pretty quickly. Egypt lived in the rear apartment with her Mom. She was eight years my senior but acted as if she was at least 40. She never seemed to have time for the people in the neighborhood who were her age. It appeared she may have thought she was better than the neighborhood girls. But, as she would say, "I ain't got time to be bullshittin'." She would hang out with women from the other part of town, like Burgess Place or Linden Street, who worked at beauty salons and bars, and who drove cars.

I was very attracted to her. She was not the prettiest girl I had ever seen, but she was certainly the sexiest. Her thick black hair was always worn in a short modern-type hairstyle. She had the most beautiful brown eyes. They were narrow in shape, and very bright. When she looked at me when I spoke to her, it seemed like she could see right through me. Her smooth, almond-colored skin was unblemished and radiant. Egypt's full lips were always moist. They were just a shade lighter than her complexion and seemed to be in constant kissing position, which gave even more appeal to her beautiful pearly white teeth. Her taut shoulders and voluptuous breasts gave way to her sexy, not-so-flat stomach, and blended very well with her round, shapely behind and long athletic, slightly bowlegs. With her head tilted just slightly to the side, her slow sensuous walk resembled an exotic runway model.

I would always flirt with Egypt every chance I got, saying corny things like, "Damn, Egypt you must be the reason for this beautiful day we are having," and "God has definitely sent you down here on Earth to tease man, to show us what we are missing up in Heaven." She would just smile and say, "Little boy you better go 'head." I would always say what I thought seemed to be the wrong thing to Egypt, or any other girl, for that matter. But I was so attracted to Egypt that I tried everything.

One evening I had been looking out the window trying to feel the cool breeze of that summer night when I noticed Egypt walking her mother to a waiting taxi. The sexy tangerine sundress she wore flowed in the summer breeze as she assisted her Mom. It was exactly that moment that I decided to give this opportunity my best shot.

After safely putting her Mom in the taxi, she turned to head back to the building. I ran to my apartment door, and when I opened it, she was just past it.

I calmly called her name, yet my heart was racing a mile a minute. She turned toward me, with that very sexy smile on her face. She said, "What boy?!" I went in! "Listen Egypt, I really don't like being a pain in the ass to you," I said in my best Billy Dee Williams voice, But I think that you are a very sexy and beautiful woman, and although I am a little younger than you ....(I paused) looking her directly in the eyes, I am so attracted to you. I mean, I don't know if you have a man, and, for real-for real, I'm not even sure if that matters to me. All I know Baby is that I dig you, and I am just needing you to give me the opportunity to show you that you will dig me back," I said smiling.

Her silence was paralyzing. The hallway, in which we were standing, seemed to get a little darker than usual. The fading grey walls slowly closed in on me. The flickering dim light bulb appeared ready to burst. My heart pounded against my chest, and I began to sweat buckets as I awaited her response. Calmly, and so very sexily, she turned, walking away from me, reached backward to take my hand (like a quarterback passes a football off to his receiver) and says in a voice so softly, "Let's go inside my house." My whole body felt like a giant firecracker. I wanted to scream "YES!!!!!" and pump my in the air fist right then and there. But I held my composure and followed Egypt into her apartment.

Although I thought I was cool, Egypt sensed my nervousness. After we walked through the door, she turned to me, standing very close, looking up into my eyes and whispered, "Don't be nervous." She stood on her toes to kiss me gently on my lips. First one, then another, and another before she eased her soft sugary tongue into my mouth. I kind of held it gently between my lips at first, enjoying the hot sweet taste of it until she began to caress my face and entire head, easing it deeper into my waiting mouth. I rolled my tongue around hers, slowly, methodically, while I pulled her closer to me, caressing, massaging, and savoring the feel of her heated body.

As we explored every inch of each other's bodies with nearly all our senses, a cyclone of pleasure overtook me.

I began to push myself deeper and deeper into Egypt, holding myself there for about two seconds with each passion-filled thrust until I exploded in indescribable ecstasy. But Egypt sweetly reached up to take my face between her hands and positioned my ear so close to her mouth that I could feel her soft lips brush against it. She reassured me that everything would be okay and that we had plenty of time.

I smiled to myself thinking of how comfortable she made me feel. As the sweat dripped down from my face onto hers, Egypt would utter things in between breaths that fueled the fire inside me. "You fit so perfectly inside me. I love the way you fill me up. Yessss, that's it, right there Baby." I was in Human Heaven! I had never imagined having sex could be so fulfilling. I devoured her, slowly, hungrily, and without pause or shame. Over, and over again.

Experiencing her (including who she was as a person) was a far cry from anything I had ever experienced. Everything I knew about people, especially women, was that they were callous, manipulating, insincere, and hostile. I mean, the initial exterior of some people may have been cordial or polite, but once exposed to them for any length of time, I would usually find them to be mischievous and underhanded with ill intent. However, Egypt was the opposite, in every way: kind, caring, genuine, and loving.

I lay there in the middle of her queen-sized bed, on cloud nine. Her warm soft body lay partially on top of mine, one leg over my hip, her foot dangling between my legs, her arm across my chest, and her face nestled between my chin and shoulder. I could feel her warm breath and soft lips on my neck as she slept. There was no place in the world I would have rather been than right there, with her.

"Reesee!!!!" My Momma walked up and down the hall, yelling, "Reesee!!!!", shattering the euphoric scene. I jumped outta bed and gathered my things together as fast as I could. "I'm sorry," I shamefully expressed to Egypt. "My Momma be buggin'," I offered. "It's alright," Egypt assured.

As I rushed to put on my clothes, I could see Egypt out of my peripheral, smiling. I wondered what she was thinking. Once I was dressed, I turned to her and said, "Thank you." She looked a bit puzzled by my words. She sat up with her legs crossed in front of her in the middle of the bed, her look softened, and the most beautiful smile enveloped her face as she cooed, "Thank you too."

I turned to walk towards the door feeling like the luckiest boy in the world. The smile on my face was cemented. I reached the door and put my hand on the doorknob, smiling, and thought, "Is she your girlfriend?"

Without a second thought, I turned to Egypt and asked, full of glee, "Are you my girlfriend?" The smile she wore turned into complete horror. She looked at me as if my head was engulfed in flames. She had no words, just a look of utter disbelief. Deflated and embarrassed, I opened the door and walked out. That was my last encounter with Egypt.

"I need you to go cross the screet to Shatzmen Hardware Sto and get me a few of dem black plastic bags. I want you to get the scrong ones, the heavy ones, so you can put some of these clothes in there that's laying round. And once you put dem clothes in da bag, I want you to put da bags in da closet so I can walk through my damn house. Don't make no sense, all these clothes just laying all over the place," Momma orated, as she pushed four quarters in my hand.

I figured I would get the bags for my Momma, put the clothes in the bag, and then get back to Egypt's house. But as soon as I walked outta Shatzman's Hardware Store, I literally walked right into Randy, Chauncy, Don, Gary and Marlen. "Yo, pardon me," I stammered. I immediately poked my chest out (a non-verbal way of saying I ain't scared). I kept walking across the street. Randy barked, "You better watch where the fuck you going, you fucking bum!" They all chuckled. I looked back at them. I was so angry, my head felt like it was about to burst from anger. My body felt hot, and my vision began to blur. However, I was not stupid, not this day. I knew had I responded, I would have gotten my ass tore up right in front of my building. So, I kept it moving. As I was about to walk into my building, I saw Claud (Hasim) Douglas walking out of Rodriquez Grocery store on the corner. Hasim was my dude. We both grew up Downtown. He was a tall, skinny, light-skinned dude with red freckles, but he had the heart of a lion when it came to crime. He was wild and not afraid to get money, a little violent in the commission of the capers, but he got the money, nonetheless.

"Raheem, what up man?!" He called cheerfully. "Yo!! Hasim, what's up wit you, man?! What you doing up here?!" "You know I go where the money at, man." He boasted. "Well, where it's at, Nigga?" I questioned. "Let's go, Nigga. Think I'm bullshittin!?" he chuckled. I didn't think Has was bullshittin'. In fact, I knew better. Whenever Has said there is money to be made, you could bet your mother's rent money that it was true. "Hold up a minute," I said, before darting in the house without my momma noticing, threw the bag on the table, and shot right back outside. "Let's go Nigga," I declared cheerfully.

We walked down towards Lexington Avenue, smoking cigarettes and talking shit. We talked about Third Street and all the people we had robbed. Hasim was funny as fuck. He'd found something to laugh about in almost anything.

For example, we were talking about the time we robbed the landlord of some building one night. It was around the first of the month, so the landlord would walk from apartment to apartment collecting the rent money. Hasim came by my house late one night and told me, "Raheem, I got one." All I wanted to know was when, and where.

We had caught the dude in the alley putting the money in the inside pocket of his trench coat. We surprised him, obviously, because when dude looked up and saw us, he looked like an albino deer caught in headlights. I rushed the dude, knocking him down to the ground. Hasim immediately searched the inside of the guy's coat looking for the pocket with the bread in it. He couldn't locate the pocket, so he started ferociously kicking and stomping the dude in the face, growling, "Where's the money, Where's the money!" Hasim already knew where the money was but couldn't get to the pocket for some reason. So, Hasim decided to rip the whole coat with the money in it off the dude. And he continued to pummel him. Hasim recalled, huddled over in laughter, "Every time I stomped or punched him, he made that sound like the Pillsbury Dough Boy, 'Whoohoo'," Hasim laughed. Has was hilarious, in a dark kind of way.

As we turned down President Street, Hasim directed my attention to a tall white man pulling down a security gate of a store. Hasim whispered to me in a low, mischievous tone, "See that brown sack by his foot? That's where all the money he made today is." Before I even had a chance to focus on the sack, Hasim had run across the street, pushed the man against the gate, and pressed his 007 knife against the man's neck. "Empty yo pockets muthafucka!" Has demanded. I had already secured the sack, yet Has, with this nefarious grin on his face, continued to press the knife onto the man's neck. The man's face, filled with fear, was pale white and sweating. The man began to plead for his life, begging us to just take the sack and go. Hasim held his face an inch away from the man's face, just marveling at the fear in the man's eyes. "Let's go Nigga!" I barked, "Let's get the fuck outta here." Has held the man up and kneed him in the nuts, hard, about three times before letting him fall to the ground. "Muthafucka!" Hasim spat at the man, as we ran away.

Like always, Has was right. There was well over a thousand dollars in the sack. He and I got high all day and talked shit to each other until we decided to split up after we noticed the police were flooding the area looking for us. The next day, either by a description of me by the robbed guy or witness, or by a stool pigeon report of me flaunting the bread that I had, the police found their way to my front door. I wasn't home at the time, but my sisters told me they suggested I turn myself in. "Imagine that" I thought. I felt that I would "pay up when the police caught up." I was young and felt invincible.

My Mom then set it up for me to move in with my Dad for a while, perhaps until the heat died down. I really didn't know how to feel about that, because one of my most in-depth feelings of nothingness came at the hands of my Dad.

He and my Mom had long ago gone their separate ways. From what I heard, my Dad was one of Third Street's well-known people. He was tall, good-looking, slick (in a country kind of way), dapper, and people genuinely seemed to like him. He was polite and always a gentleman. Most people respected him.

One Christmas, it was said that GeeChee Leroy was coming to the building. Everybody was talking about it. I was about eight years old. I had had no contact with him, so I was excited that I would get a chance to see him. In my head, I believed that he would come to the apartment bearing gifts, and he would swoop me up in his arms, kiss my head and tell me how much he missed and loved me. I stood at the window of our second-floor apartment for what seemed like hours with my face pushed up against the glass, waiting for him to come.

Finally, a large brown and beige station wagon pulled up and double parked in front of the building. A tall, brown-skinned, handsome man got of the passenger side wielding a brand new guitar in one hand and a bag of colorful giftwrapped packages in the other. I ran to the kitchen yelling, "Mommy, my father's here, my father's here!!" My Mom was silent and continued to wash the dishes. I could feel her occasionally look down at me with an indiscernible expression. Soon after, there was a knock on the door. I stood next to my mother, smiling, anticipating, "Come in," she welcomed, in her "I wonder who that is" voice.

In walked this phenomenal figure. Taller than he appeared from the window, and more handsome than I had imagined. If I could have thought of a word back then that would have fully described him at that moment, it would have been "Majestic". My Dad was Majestic!

As I stood there looking up into his face waiting for him to make eye contact with me, he said "Hey" to my Mom, in an indifferent tone, held the guitar and the bag out to her, with what I thought to be a look of disdain on his face, turned around and walked right back out of the door. Never even acknowledged me! I felt invisible. Yet, my heart felt like it weighed a thousand pounds. There was a huge lump in my throat and my eyes filled up with tears. I could not speak but my soul screamed: "DADDY!!! DON'T YOU SEE ME?!! DADDY, DADDY!! I'm right here, don't you see me?!!" I heard each one of his footsteps get farther and farther away as he walked down the hall, down the stairs, and out of the building. I could not bring myself to look out the window to watch him leave. I was too weak. Instead, I sank to the floor, crying and thinking, "What did I do, why he don't love me?" "Why don't he want to be my father?"

Living with my Dad was different. He and his wife lived in Aspen Place Projects, which was one of the places people from Third Street beefed with relentlessly. People from the Projects thought they were better than people from Downtown (Third Street), and people from Uptown thought they were better than both. We all beefed with each other and fought every chance we got.

At any rate, my Dad and his wife were always very nice to me and always overextended themselves to accommodate me. After about three days of living with my Dad and his wife, he had come back from the store with some lard for frying chicken. I was sitting on the couch in the living room watching Gunsmoke. He stopped to watch his favorite scene. He had probably seen this scene a thousand times. As the screen faded into commercial, my Dad sat down next to me and, in almost a whisper as he looked down at the floor, he began to tell me about an argument that he and my Mom had about a year after I was born.

He said that my Mom had been extremely drunk at the time. When she drank, she could be very, very nasty. He said she was angry with him because she thought he had been flirting with another woman. He said that she was so angry and jealous that she screamed, "That boy in there ain't yours anyway!"

He said he was speechless and looked at her in shock and disbelief. He said that he was so pissed off because he knew I was his child that he wanted to slap her. He said he stood up, pushed her to the ground and never spoke to her again. He said that he knew he could have had some communication with me, but he was so angry with her that he didn't even try. He paused for a minute, looked up at me and asked me to look at him. He said, poignantly, "Reesee, I'm sorry." I hugged him, tears rolled down my face and I said, "I understand Dad, it's okay."

My Dad always tried to make me feel comfortable. The idea was for me to be exposed to different people and a different way of living. I suspect that he just hoped I'd blend in. However, I felt out of place with the people from the Projects, and, at my Dad's house, in that setting, where I was supposed to feel "at home," I felt very uncomfortable. I was used to just flopping where I wanted to sit, leaving my clothes on the floor, drinking out of the water bottle in the fridge and scrounging around in the kitchen trying to find something to eat.

There, at my Dad's house, food was plentiful, and I could eat anything (in reason) at any time, I was told to use a glass to drink out of, to put my clean clothes in the drawer and my dirty clothes in the dirty clothes hamper. What?! "Dirty clothes hamper, drawer?!" I thought. We had a big black garbage bag at my Mom's house that we put all our clothes in, no matter dirty or clean. We simply held them up to see if there were any recognizable stains and smelled them to see if they stunk to determine if they were dirty or clean.

At my dad's, I felt like I was always being watched and corrected. And although my Dad's wife tried to be nice to me, she always had her nose turned up when she would talk to me...like she was annoyed or bothered. I was more comfortable running the street. Before long, I was back Downtown hanging with the people that I was used to. I basically used my Dad's place to sleep and change clothes.

My focus was weed, beer, and pills. I got high all the time. As a result, I began to steal from my Dad and his wife. They could not put anything down without me stealing it. I even stole my Dad's wife's wedding ring. While she and her sisters played cards in the living room, I eased in the bedroom and rummaged through her things. I wasn't looking for the ring specifically, I was looking for anything of value. However, when I saw it, I took it, didn't give it a second thought.

At that point in my life, I was so wrapped up in trying to run away from what I felt and thought about me and my life, that nothing else mattered except more drugs. Drugs provided for me an invaluable escape from my reality. In fact, for the most part, I made a conscious effort not to think about how I or anybody else felt. I was angry all the time. And, all that I knew was that I hated seeing my Mom drunk and passed out all the time, I hated thinking about my Dad being absent at the times in my life that I needed him most, I hated seeing my Dad drunk, disoriented, and violent with his wife; who was an amputee and wore an artificial leg. The confusion about why my family (Mom and sisters) seemed to live in the worse conditions of anybody I had known infuriated me, and the horror of brutal, disgusting, and shameful things Broom Hilda did to me stalked my every waking moment. I didn't want to think, I didn't want to remember, I didn't want to feel, and I didn't want to be me.

My grandma (my Dad's Mom) loved me to no end. Dad had sent me to live with my grandma, grandpa, and uncle in the next building at the behest of his wife, I'm sure. She knew I had stolen her wedding ring. One evening while my Dad was out, she asked me if I remembered when she showed me where her jewelry was. I said yes, (not thinking) because she had never shown me where her jewelry was. She just looked at me with disgust and disdain in her eyes and walked away from me. She rarely said a word to me after that.

My grandma was welcoming, and I could tell by the way she talked to me that she wanted to fix me. I guess she thought that if I was given the abundance of love that she was giving me, I would be ok. She used to hold me and stroke my head and tell me that everything would be alright. She gave me whatever I asked for and demanded that Grandpa and my Uncle Pooh do the same. However, there was a beast residing inside of me that I could not tame. It had no conscience and no control. It was relentless in achieving its goal to get high. I broke her heart, countless times. I stole from her, lied to her and embarrassed her.

I remember one warm summer day, standing in front of the building. Everyone hung in front of their building in the Projects on a nice summer day. My Grandma got out of a cab, coming from a church function. I rushed up to the cab door to help her with her bags. But she snatched her bags away and looked at me in a way that I had never seen. Her eyes were red, filled with tears and anger. Her top lip was curled up with venom as she spat: "I wish you change yo fucken last name, so I don't have keep explaining to all my damn friends at church why my grandson's name is always in the fucken newspaper!" She walked away, leaving me with my mouth wide open. I didn't know what to say. I couldn't think of why my name would be in a recent newspaper article. I mean, I hadn't been busted lately. I was baffled. I could hear the disappointment every time she spoke to me after that day. I knew my grandma was hurt and had finally lost the grace she had given me and the faith she had in me changing.

My grandma died a few years later from emphysema. By that time, I was running so hard, I didn't even attend the funeral. The day after her funeral however, I remember sitting on the stoop of someone's house (in a moment of clarity) thinking how sorry I was for doing all the things I had done to break her heart, and how I would never get the chance to tell her in person how much I sincerely regretted the things I had done. Never again able to tell her how much I loved her. Never able to apologize sincerely. In my heart, I wished there was a way for my Grandma to hear my words, or even look into my heart and know that I never intentionally meant to cause her pain or embarrassment. That it was the unwelcome beast in my spirit and mind that controlled my every action.

Although I did not know the full nature of addiction at that time, I did know however, that no matter how hard I did not want to do some of the things I did, I did them anyway because I felt it was who I was. I had completely bought into: "You sneaky, you grimy, you dirty and dumb. You almost nothing." However, from the bottom of my heart, and from the depths of my soul, I needed her to know how truly sorry I was/am to have been such a disappointment. At that time, no one had ever shown me as much love as my Grandma did.

\\

CHAPTER 8

Follow your heart, but take your good sense with you

By the time I was 18 I had moved out on my own. Well, actually, a friend from the old neighborhood named Billy and I had rented a furnished room. Billy worked at Center Diner from 10 p.m. to 7 a.m. So, I jumped at the opportunity to go half with him on the room. Not only because I would have the room to myself most of the time, but because Billy had a job. That meant that if I ever had a problem getting my half of the rent, I could count on Billy to pick up the slack until I got my hands on someone else's money to pay him back.

I respected Billy a great deal. He and I grew up together under some of the same circumstances. Yet, he never got in trouble with the law, always kept a job or hustle, was very responsible with everything, and the girls loved him. He was a medium-sized dude and kind of meek in personality. Over the years I grew to love this dude like a biological brother, because despite my antics and ill ways of thinking, he still accepted me for who I was and always without hesitation had my back when I needed him most. And I, like a true brother, had his in return.

I met a young lady named Cutie shortly after we rented the furnished room. She was one of the finest young women that lived in Aspen Place Projects. She was 24, short, thick, brown-skinned, and had the sexiest mouth I had ever seen. Her lips were big and brown and smooth, and very soft. Her tongue looked as soft as a pink sugary cloud. When she talked, I couldn't help staring at her mouth. And like magic, without fail, I'd become as hard as a slumlord on rent day. She was beautiful.

I met her in the elevator one day when I was headed to my Dad's house to visit. We got on the elevator at the same time. She lived on the 8th floor, my dad lived on the 7th. "Damn, you handsome!" she said mischievously. "I ain't never seent you around here. Where you going?" "By my Dad's house," I answered in my deepest voice. "Who you Dad?" "Leroy," I announced proudly. "Oh, okay. I ain't know Leroy had a son that look like you!" She grinned. "Here, take my phone number and call me when you get in the house," she said confidently.

On our first date, I found myself in New York on 116th Street asking an older woman whose hands were as big as catchers' mitts if she knew where I could find a half quarter of "Black Tape" dope. She directed me to a building on the corner of Morningside, on the 3rd floor. I headed up there with Cutie in tow. She suggested that I get a whole quarter, which I did.

I fell in love with dope that day. From that day on, dope and Cutie became my reasons for getting up in the morning. I found myself doing some of the craziest shit. Not only to get dope, but also to keep money to keep Cutie. She wore only the latest and nicest shit, and she had no problem with letting me know that she expected me to help her continue wearing that kind of shit.

In return, she sucked my soul right of my body every chance she got. She'd wake me up early in the morning with my dick in her mouth. She'd suck it in bathroom if Billy was home, on the elevator in her building when I'd walk her home, and even in the exit. And Cutie pretty much taught me everything I knew about how to please a woman. "Every woman ain't the same Raheem," she cautioned. "You have to read a woman's reaction to what you are doing to her. If it feels good to her, continue to do it. But if her body, voice, or words are not saying what you are doing feels good, you must explore her body to find what does feels good to her."

She was unlike any teacher I had ever had on any subject. She was patient, complimentary, excited when I did something exactly right, and never condescending when I missed the mark. She told me that, "a big dick don't make you good in bed," "It's the way you work that big muthafucka that matters most," she would say almost poignantly. "It also has a whole lot to do with what you make a woman feel before giving her all that dick. You gotta make her want it and be willing to endure the pain it might bring. So, you kiss her, touch her, look at her like there is no one else, and you gotta know how to eat that pussy the way she like it done. Cause everybody is different, Raheem." She intended to teach me well.

After a while, I used to enjoy watching her catch her breath while trying to tell me I was the best she ever had. Her only problem, if there was one, was that she loved to sniff dope. No one could tell this by looking at her; as I said, she was flawless.

One night on our way back from Tony's Pizza on Main Avenue, Cutie, Billy, and I saw a man standing in front of the Wonder Bar counting a bunch of money. I had been yearning for dope all day. So, at Cutie's request, I began to plot on how to rob this dude. He was old, about 40, but he was a big dude, and I knew I'd need some help. "Billy, help me get this muthafucka!" I demanded. Shocked that I would even consider asking him such a question, he kind of just stood there looking at me like I had lost my damn mind. Billy was not criminally inclined. There was never a time that I have known him not have a job.

The yearning for the dope had gott"n st'onger now that I saw all the money, and I really didn't think too much more about what Billy thought. "You gone help me or what Nigga?" I questioned, irritated. As Billy walked off, disgusted with me, I told Cutie to catch up with him and meet me at the room. I grabbed a big piece of wood that had been leaning on the trash can, ran up behind the dude, and struck him on the head hard with the wooden stick. The man hit the ground like a cinderblock. I grabbed all of the money from his stiff hand and ran all the way to Columbia Avenue.

When I got to the room, Cutie was in the bathroom. I began to boast to Billy about having knocked the dude out, while counting out $720 on the dresser. Billy looked at me in contempt, with pity in his eyes. Empathetically Billy announced, "You need help man. You all strung out on that shit man. I have seen people go to those drug programs and get help from psych doctors as well as help with drug problems. You need some help before you kill somebody or somebody gonna kill you. Yo ass going to one of them drug places tomorrow to get help or I'm moving the fuck outta here, man." "Yeah, Yeah, Yeah," I replied, seemingly unphased by what he said, as I left out the room to get Cutie and head down to the dope spot.

While walking, I gave Cutie the money to hold, except the $40 needed to cop. She always suggested she hold my money when I had an abundance of it because with money, I was usually impetuous and overly generous. In my haste to get down to the dope spot, I never even thought to change my clothes. My stomach was bubbling and all I could think of was grooving.

After copping, Cutie and I stopped in the hallway of the building to take a hit. As soon I snorted the powdery white substance my stomach instantly felt better, and I didn't think about anything else except getting back to the room to be comfortable while we nodded.

As we exited the spot, the police were right there. Guns drawn. Multiple demands were shouted for me to get down on the ground as they surrounded me. Cutie kept walking. Someone had obviously seen the whole robbery scene and gave a description of me to the police. Billy didn't have to worry about me going to get help the next day. If there was any help for me it would have to wait, because that night I was taken to jail for robbery. A few months later I was sentenced to seven years in Annandale Correctional Facility.

I spent two years in Annandale. The experience there was pretty much the same as Jamesburg. Same people, different faces. It didn't really phase me. I had accepted going to jail as part of my life. I was pretty much in jail more than I was in society.

The only difference with this time was that I had a huge attachment to Cutie. I thought about her all the time. I wrote her letters, but she never wrote back. I called her phone, but no one ever accepted the charges. I often wondered if she even got the letters I sent. "Surely, she would have written me back," I thought.

Cutie was my first "Girlfriend." And I'm sure she didn't know her family had the phone fixed in a way that my collect calls wouldn't go through. Something had to be wrong. Yet, I continued to write to her and call her house, hoping that I'd eventually get through. I never did.

When I was released from Annandale, the first place I went to was Cutie's house. She was never home. I visited several more times, but she would never be there. Her cousin Kendell said she hadn't been home in days. I was worried about her.

That weekend I went to the town's hot spot bar, Sugar Bill's, looking for her. As soon as I entered the spot, my eyes focused on a chick who looked just like Cutie. However, this couldn't be, because a short, brown-skinned, mismatched-color-wearing dude had a yard of tongue down this girl's throat. But as soon as he allowed the chick to breathe, she looked up and our eyes met. Sure 'nuff, it was Cutie. My heart stopped, then started beating a thousand beats a minute. Angry, excited, and confused, I started walking towards them. "Somebody is 'bout to tell me what the fuck is going on!" I thought. As quickly as I walked toward them, she walked towards me. As she got closer to me, she extended her arms and palms out and backed me up.

"What the fuck was that?" I questioned, angrily. "Oh, don't worry about that, that's Poopi. He's Cuban." She offered, nonchalantly. "Who the fuck is…." "That's just my friend," she interrupted, "You got any dope?" she inquired. No explanation, no apologies, no "I missed you". Nothing, except "You got any dope?" I stood there staring at her, astonished, for a few seconds, not knowing what to make of this. My mind was going in a thousand different directions at a thousand miles an hour.

Finally, I turned and walked away from her, confused, disappointed and angry. I later found out Poopi was hustling coke and was her new boyfriend. She had moved in with him, which is why she never stayed at her mother's house.

I was in physical pain. I wanted to find a dark corner, curl up and just cry. I couldn't figure out why this happened. She said she loved me. She said that I was the best boyfriend she ever had. She said that she would always be in my corner whenever I needed her. She said....

It hit me like a ton of bricks. All the women In my life had been liars. Liars, moved by sex, alcohol and drugs. If you gave them sex, they lied and said they loved you; if you gave them alcohol they wouldn't say they love you and they didn't care what you did to them, or with other people; and if you gave them drugs, they'd let you do whatever you wanted to them, they'd say they love you, they would pretend to care about your well-being, until the next person with more drugs came along. "Bitches," I thought. "I'll never give a fuck about nan 'nutha one as long as I live. All they do is use people: use people and lie.

CHAPTER 9

It ain't what they say, it's what they do

I ran into Eddie Townsand that night, a childhood friend, up bar called The Oak Inn. "Hey Raheem, what up man?" he cheered, genuinely happy to see me. "I'm good man, just got out today. So, I'm chilling," "Yo," Eddie announced, I got two girls lined up, ready to fuck. I just need somebody to handle the fat one." He smiled. "You wit it?!" Actually, I would have been "wit" fucking a blowup doll at that point. My heart was broken; I was angry, confused, and horny as hell. Besides, I thought, "Here's my opportunity to give these Bitches a taste of their own medicine. I'ma fuck and suck her brains out and never set eyes on her fat ass again." "Hell yeah, I'm down. Where they at?!"

"Yo Baby, what's up?" I inquired as I floated up close to them. "How y'all doing" I asked, smiling a big bright smile. "I'm fine," the fat one announced. "Fine is definitely what y'all is," I lied. The one Eddie was trying to woo looked like a snail without the shell. She was tall and slim like a spaghetti box... no breasts or butt, just long arms and legs which were knock-kneed and pigeon-toed. She was a butterscotch color with a dull complexion. She had a small round head, wore a short natural hair style, and big hoop earrings. However, she had big pink, very soft looking lips. Eddie claimed she could suck the paint off the wall. Andrea was her name.

"My name is Raheem, what's your name, Baby?" The fat one announced gleefully, "My name is Kathy, but you can call me Kat." She was a cute girl. Just a bit rotund, I thought. She was light-complexioned, with pretty, light brown eyes and thick black hair, which she wore in loose curls. She had broad shoulders and a wide, flat ass. She was built like a helicopter. But that pretty face and wet-looking mouth made her body almost unimportant. She also revealed she was 10 years older than me. However, that didn't seem to matter to me or her. I mentioned at some point that I had just got home from jail. Her face lit up like a big red Santa Claus Christmas tree ornament!

About an hour later, Kat and I were en route to her place. We didn't talk much on our way to her apartment or even after we got there. We both knew what we wanted. We got to it immediately. I had intended on just doing my thing and leaving. But once I got started, "doing my thing" took on a whole other meaning. I mean, I was still angry at Cutie, and absolutely took it out on Kat sexually. I pounded this woman in every position I could think of. And when she'd ask to take a break I'd say, "just two more minutes Baby," then pound her even harder. I thoroughly explored every orifice. We fucked, laughed, and sniffed coke and dope till at least 9 in the morning.

Needless to say, that night Kat had become my girlfriend. Yeah, I know what I said to myself earlier, but shit, Kat was something else. I had even introduced her to my family. She was funny, high- spirited, and initially my family seemed to like her too.

However, as we began to get to know her, she would make up absurd stories, out of the blue. She once told my mother that there was a milk and eggs shortage in the world. And, if things didn't get better soon, the world would resort to goat's milk and turkey eggs. I was floored. I mean, I stayed watching the news and I had never heard of no shit like that. I looked at her like: "What the fuck?!" But she continued on as if what she was saying was the gospel truth. My sister Dee Dee, who has no filter, finally said, "Raheem, this Bitch crazy." I wanted to explode in laughter at what my sister said so bluntly. But out of embarrassment I announced that we had to go.

I found that Kat lied like that all the time, for no obvious reason, which was irritating. So basically, our relationship dwindled to something based solely on sex and drugs. But to my surprise, Kat announced she was pregnant. And I was ecstatic at the thought that I would be a parent. I told my Mom and sisters about the news, thinking they would be as happy as I was. But they all asked the same question: "Are you sure she pregnant?" I knew how they could ask that question, but I just couldn't imagine someone making something like that up. It turned out; she was pregnant.

After about three months, Hasim and I had gotten knocked off again for a bullshit robbery that got downgraded to a larceny. I did about nine months in the County Jail before I took a plea deal. They didn't have the gun, so I copped to a four flat. While I was there, I would occasionally talk to my sister on the phone; she made it clear they believed the baby boy Kat had was not mine. They all said the baby did not look like me at all.

However, I did not want to believe that. When I was paroled out, I rushed over to Kat's apartment to see my son. The child did not look like me but, "He just looks more like his mother," I thought. I asked her directly, "Is this my son?" "Yes," she replied excitedly. "Look at him! That's all you!"

That's all I needed to hear. Because I needed something/someone to love. I needed someone to pour into what I wanted to believe real love was. I wanted to show my son what a good present Dad is supposed to be, what a nurturing Dad did for his son. I wanted to build his confidence and show him the integrity and self-acceptance that I never had. But more than anything else, I wanted someone to love me for me.

We continued fucking and sucking like nothing had changed. One morning, Kat, with my son in her lap, and I were sitting in the living room watching TV. Her other three children were playing in the back room when there was a knock on the door. I went to the door and opened it without asking who it was. In walked Parker Brooks. Parker was of the hood. I mean, he was known to be a good fighter and was respected. He even sold dope for a minute. I had heard he was in the County Jail for a couple of months, but I didn't know why he was knocked off. But he and I were cool, and I already knew Kat knew and was cool with a lot of people. So, there was no reason for pause or concern when he showed up at the house. "Yo Man, what's up Parker?" I announced, happy to see him.

"Raheem," he replied, smiling, with a firm handshake hug. "How you bro?" "I'm good, man. When you touch down?" I asked. "This morning," he declared with a relieved and happy chuckle. "Where's Kat?" he asked excitedly. "She's in there man, go ahead," I directed, as I walked behind him.

The look on her face when Parker walked through the door was one of fear, desperation, and confusion, framed in a shaky smile. "Hhh..Hey Parker," she stammered, "When you get home?" she tried to sound excited while holding the nervous smile in place. "This morning," he said, with the same happy tone while reaching for my son in Kat's lap. The look on Kat's face turned into absolute terror.

"What the fuck is happening?" I thought, until Parker held my son in his arms, cheek to cheek. I nearly passed out. My body began to feel like it was boiling inside. I began to sweat, I felt lightheaded, and my knees began to wobble as I watched the words, "Who is this handsome little dude?" come out of his mouth in slow motion. Parker held my son in his arms looking at him in astonishing pride. My son and Parker Brooks were the spitting image of each other. Undeniable. I walked out of the house not really knowing how to feel. I mean, I was angry that Kat had me believing the child was mine, but I also felt a deep sense of loss. I knew at that point that I couldn't continue to care for and love this child the way that I wanted to. I wanted to give this child all of the things that I craved as a child growing up. I wanted to teach him to be the man I hoped to become one day: independent, strong responsible, respected and accomplished. I also immediately began to mourn what I thought was the best sex in the world. Then, I thought, "You done let another Bitch get you again, Raheem."

CHAPTER 10

Just because it looks good TO you, doesn't mean it's good FOR you...

I moved back into my mother's apartment. Billy's Mom lived in the same building. I hadn't seen him since I got home from Annandale. I ran into him one day in the hallway. He was happy to see me. He kept shaking my hand and telling me how tall I had gotten and how I didn't look like dirty little Raheem anymore.

We laughed, hard. We reminisced about the old days growing up. We talked about Cutie and how strung out I was over her, and we laughed for a long while. I told him what had happened with Kat. He didn't seem surprised, and I didn't question his reaction. He obviously heard about it already or knew something about the person Kat was. We talked about the new bar that opened on Main Avenue called DJ's. He said all the fly honeys hung out there. Uptown, Downtown, honeys from the Projects, and Paterson would be there. "Kool," I said excitedly. "I'll see you there tonight."

I put on my thick, beige corduroy pants, with a burgundy and beige button-up shirt, burgundy penny loafer shoes, soft-looking beige wool sports jacket, and burgundy applejack Kangol hat. I sprayed on a little Grey Flannel cologne and headed out the door to DJ's.

The music was loud and there was wall to wall women all the way to the pool table. I placed my quarters on the table, ordered a Lowenbrau beer, and kind of leaned against the wall to wait for my time to play. I scanned the bar looking for Billy. He was in the corner near the ladies' room talking to a short pretty girl with a huge, round, perfectly shaped ass. He looked up over his Gazelle glasses and gave me the peace sign.

I laughed inwardly, remembering the shy little dude he used to be. When it was my turn to play, I floated up to the table displaying my most confident walk. When I kneeled to gather and rack the balls, a soft sexy voice whispered in my ear, "You look very nice Raheem. How are you?" I smiled, looked up to respond and was more than delighted to see Lidia Whitfield standing there.

Her voluptuous, red lipstick-covered, soft-looking, sexy lips smiled back at me. Her short sexy hair style accentuated her perfect round face and caramel-colored skin. I had always been attracted to Lidia but had been intimidated because of her age. I was 20 and she was about 28 or 29. I'd see her all the time either riding past my Mom's apartment building, or in #11 School Park hanging out with her friend Bridgette. She'd always smile and speak.

In my sexiest Billy Dee Williams voice, looking directly into her light brown eyes I said: "I'm fantastic, young lady, how are you." She giggled a shy girlish laugh. "Go ahead and play your game, Raheem. We'll talk when you're finished", she smiled. Man, I ain't never lost a game of pool so fast in my life. I walked over to her at the bar and asked her if she'd like to have a drink. "I'd rather dance," she coyly replied.

Dennis Edwards' *"Don't Look Any Further"* blared from the huge speakers as we tore the dance floor up.

She had the tendency to sing the song aloud and look me in the eyes as she danced. All I could think about as we danced was how long I had been waiting to get this close to her. After we danced to several songs, we sat at the bar. We talked and laughed for what seemed to be only minutes when the DJ announced, "Last call for alcohol, last call for alcohol." We looked at each other awkwardly for a moment. I did not know if I should ask to go back to her apartment or what.

"Here's my number," interrupted my thoughts, as she pushed a matchbook in my hand. "You can call me when you want to, ok? I'll see you some other time." "Um... Um...," not knowing what to say. Finally, "Alright Sweetheart, I'll see you some other time," forcing a smile.

I looked around for Billy to secure my ride home. I learned that he had left an hour earlier with a young lady. Suddenly a light went off inside my head. I waited across the street in the 24-hour Dunkin Donuts, estimating just enough time for Lidia to get home before I called her.

"Hey Lidia, you ain't gonna believe this. My honcho Billy stepped off with some chick with my coat in his car. I'm standing out here cold as hell with no coat on. But I'm thinking maybe I can come over to your house and wait for him until he gets back, maybe call a cab or something since you only live a few blocks away." She laughed, loud. After playing hard to get for a few minutes, she relented and allowed me to come over. That night of sex with Lidia was fantastic. She was by far, at that point, neck and neck to the best sex I ever had.

As we began to see each other more, I realized she was a "Headologist," which meant she was amazingly skilled at giving head and, she appeared to love it. She said she had an oral fixation, where she enjoyed having things in her mouth. I loved it. She called it "Goodies." She loved it. I ended up moving in with her.

Unfortunately, I had a robbery beef pending. Six months later I was going to be sentenced. I never asked her if she would come to visit or write because I figured it was a gift. Especially considering the fact that she told me loved me. Shit. She even cried the night before I went in to be sentenced.

I spent 18 months in Annandale. She visited me twice, sent me $20 dollars, wrote to me three times, and sent me the summer clothes I had left at her house in the dead of winter. After about four months of being in Annandale, I never heard from her again until I came home.

She was deeply involved with a guy named Freddy, who was a short, dirty, monkey-looking fellow that always smelled of spoiled meat and old onions. He was extremely paranoid that I would come to get her back. But I did not want her back. I liked to kiss too much to want her back. The thought of Freddy's piece in her mouth was enough to always keep me at least 3 feet away. I used to see them out at local bars, chillin'. She would occasionally look in my direction, smiling. He would often catch her and then start to ice grill me. But I never face fought the guy. I simply chuckled and looked away.

One night I had been hanging out with my friend Wally McKinsey smoking angel dust outside Market Street Tavern, a bar on Third Street. When I walked back in the bar, it was clear to see that I was zooted. Freddy walked up to me and (it appeared) he screamed something. It sounded like he was underwater. "What," I asked, in my zooted slumber. He repeated the same scream and walked toward the door. I followed him.

As soon as I got outside of the Tavern's exit, he again shouted something I did not comprehend, but this time he made a slicing gesture against my neck. Before I realized what he did, he shouted again with an additional slicing motion. When I finally put my hand on my neck to see what he had done, I had lost so much blood, I fainted.

I was awakened by this dude gnawing on my thumb and growling like a dog. Someone pulled him off of me. And the next thing I remembered was waking up in the hospital.

After I got stitched up, I left the hospital and went home to put on my war uniform (sweat hood and boots) and hunted his ass down. I kicked in and jumped through Lidia's windows (thinking he was there) and I attempted to set the hallway of his building where he lived on fire. I caught him one day walking down the street and chased him into a police car with a knife in my hand. I stalked him at his job, tried to run him over with a van, and even waited outside of his house.

He finally went to the police station and signed a complaint against me and got a restraining order. I really didn't want to go back to jail so soon. But I figured we would handle this beef the way it started... In the streets. But once he got them people involved, I figured I'd blindside him one day when he least expected it, like he did me.

I was 22 with nothing on my mind except money, women and drugs. I was angry all the time. I really didn't know why. But I felt like the world owed me something. I kept thinking I was dealt a bad hand in life. Sexually abused, emotionally stunted, poverty- stricken, lied to, taken for granted. I had nothing in my favor, except a big, black, funky dick and a willingness to use people. So, nothing else seemed to matter.

I started hanging out with Jahad, a guy I knew from the old neighborhood. Jahad was kind of a country dude. I mean, not country in style, but country in the way he talked. He had that southern twang that the women seemed to love. I think some women even equated that countryness to being slow. But Jahad was far from that. Granted, he was a trick (I used to call him Trick Dawson), he didn't mind paying for pussy. Be it with drugs or money. And he wasn't known to be much of a fighter, but nobody really fucked with him, probably due to his older brother Zulu's reputation.

Jahad usually ended up with the bigger part of any kind of deal. He knew how to run his mouth. He was into selling drugs, using coke, and ran around with a lot of women, which was right up my alley. We would go to hotels almost every night with women and usually rented one room together to get high and fuck these women all night. If one of us wasn't pleased with the woman we had, we would switch. Sometimes we would switch just because we could. We targeted women who used coke and did almost anything to get it, with no shame. Jahad loved it. However, most of the women we were with probably liked that shit just as much as we did.

We hung out at a local bar called The Shangri La, on Passaic Street. Jahad and I sat at the bar drinking Lowenbrau beer and talking slick. In between sells, Jahad began telling me about this woman named Denise who allegedly could suck a golf ball through a garden hose. I laughed loudly at the country expression. But I was intrigued. "Where she at?!" I asked, laughing harder. "Sitting at the front of the bar with that pink dress on." As I looked at her, I imagined what she could do with those pink soft-looking lips.

Before long, I made my way over to her. We talked for a little while and I told her about the package of good coke I had. She agreed to have me meet her at her apartment when the bar closed. I suspected she didn't want people to see us leave together because of the implications. But I was cool with that. I went back to my seat, filled Jahad in on the happenings. He laughed as she made her way out the door.

CHAPTER 11

When opportunity knocks

As I walked up Henry Street I heard a young woman call, "Raheem." Not wanting to be slowed down, I pretended not to hear her, and I continued walking. "Raheem," the voice bellowed. "Shit!!" I exclaimed under my breath and turned around apparently irritated. "Hi' how you doing?" The woman greeted me cheerfully. "I'm alright Baby," I replied, while trying to remember where I knew this woman's face from. "I saw you at the bar and somebody told me what your name is. I was gonna speak to you earlier, but by the time I was ready, you had left," she confessed. My name is Cynthia. People call me Cissy.

Now I remembered her. I had noticed this woman looking at me earlier but didn't really pay any attention to it because I thought she was with Gary Randolph, another drug dealer I knew from the neighborhood. She wasn't all that cute, kind of ordinary looking, but attractive. She was brown-skinned, a tight curly kit in her hair, little thin lips, overweight, and boring eyes. However, she wore a silk blouse, leather skirt, gold necklace around her neck and bracelets on her wrist; and the perfume she wore was intoxicating. "Yeah" I'm on my way to a friend's house." "Oh, ok, well you think I can get your number or something?" she asked confidently. "Sure Baby, but I don't have a pen with me. "I got one upstairs," she reported. Upstairs was right across the street, which beat the hell outta walking all the way to Linden Street, I thought. I probably wasn't gonna get the head I anticipated from Denise, But I was pretty confident I was about to at least get some from this girl.

When I walked into the apartment I was totally impressed. The apartment was immaculate. Too nice to be in that area, in that building. The neighborhood was not necessarily a bad one, nor the building. It just seemed the apartment belonged somewhere else. The plush living room carpet, contemporary furniture, and modern art was something I wasn't used to seeing in this area. In fact, the only place I'd ever seen something this nice was in magazines.

As she said good night to the babysitter (a little Puerto Rican girl), I just stood there looking around thinking about how well I'ma fuck this woman. I figured she obviously had something going on, and I wanted to be a part of it. How she looked physically mattered a dam to me now.

I noticed in the curio in the corner were pictures of three little girls I imagined to be her daughters, and what appeared to be a wedding picture of herself and her husband. "You're married?" I questioned, surprised. "Separated," she replied nonchalantly, looking up at me from a brown leather recliner. "Oh, I said, relieved, as I walked over to her and got down on my knees in front of her to kiss her gently on her lips a few times before I attempted to ease my tongue into her mouth. I could feel that she was pressing her lips together tightly.

"Damn," I said apologetically. "Is my breath bad Baby?" "No," she assured. "Oh, ok. So, you are just not into kissing?" "Well, I don't know how." She shyly replied. "Yeah, right," I said, in disbelief. However, I figured, before this night is over, I'd find out. "Let's go in the bedroom and get comfort......." I was not even finished my sentence, and she was in the bedroom pulling her shit off. Scared the hell outta me!

I slowly walked into the bedroom, looking at her sideways. "Is everything ok young lady? Are you expecting someone to come here soon or something?" I asked, genuinely concerned. I guess she saw the discomfort in my face. She sat down on the bed and began to explain. She said her husband had run out on her a couple of years ago. He had met and moved in with another woman after the woman had gotten pregnant. Her husband had been the only man she had ever been with. She said it was not an affectionate kind of relationship, there was no kissing or any sense of intimacy in the relationship. She said they fucked occasionally. And, when they did, she ended up pregnant. They simply stayed together for the kids' sake. She said they had three children together. However, they had not been together sexually in over two years. She said she welcomed this opportunity to be with someone else (if only sexually) to help her get past him and move on with her life.

I simulated making love to Cynthia for at least two hours. There was a whole lot of slow kissing, caressing, light hair pulling, and slow deep thrusting while I sucked and kissed her neck and lips. She came so hard and continuously at one point that she began to cry: squeezing me tightly in her heavy arms, crying a sort of

"Thank you Jesus," in an exhausted, whimpering cry. She fell asleep immediately after.

As I lay there, I almost felt bad about my intentions for Cynthia. I mean, she was not my type of woman, physically. Her confidence and willingness to take a risk at going after what she wanted was attractive. At some point during the evening, she mentioned she worked at the High School and part time at McCrory's Department Store. That was attractive too.

I guess what appealed to me most was the bread I knew I could get from her if I continued to promise her sex. It was at that point that I began to almost feel sad for myself. I began to think how cool it is to get paid for sex and/or the illusion of me being someone's boyfriend, but I also began to think: "What else are you good at, Nigga?" It took me a minute to come up with something. "Writing? Talking? Acting? What!? Stealing? Robbing? Lying?" I felt like without being good at sex, I was almost nothing.

I could almost see Broom Hilda's hard, crusty, cracked, and blood-stained lips; smell her sour, shitty breath as she held my face in her skinny hand, squeezing it, looking me dead in the eyes, whispering: "You ain't never gone be shit. You too dumb to finish school, so you ain't never gone get a job. All you know how to do is steal and lie. So, you better learn how to use that long funky dick and that stank ass mouth you carry all of them buck ass teeth in. Cause without that you gone end up dead or in jail for the rest of your worthless ass life before you reach 18." I shook my head hard to get rid of the vision. But the sound of her voice lingered in my ears.

I awoke around 11 in the morning to the sounds and giggles of children playing in the living room. Cynthia was sitting in a large brown leather chair doing one of her daughter's hair while the others were trying on different shoes they wanted to wear.

After dressing, I walked out of the bedroom to say hello to Cynthia's children. She was visibly embarrassed and rushed the children outside to play. I respected that. Once they were out the door I smiled and jokingly said, "So, I don't rate a breakfast or nothing?" She looked a bit surprised, "Oh, you want some breakfast? I can make you some." "Nah, I was just joking Baby. But if you don't mind, I could go for some toast and milk." "Okay, I'll make you some," she mumbled.

I noticed Cynthia never looked at me. In fact, it appeared she avoided even looking in my direction. I figure she must be a little embarrassed about last night's events. So, I ate fast, gave her my number, and said goodbye.

I thought about Cynthia on my way home. She appeared to be a "Good Girl." She was obviously a good mother. She kept an immaculate apartment, and she worked two jobs. I thought that was an amazing thing. So, I figured I'd stay close and make the best of this situation and see where it would go. I stopped at the flower store on the corner of Main and Passaic Street and sent her an arraignment of flowers. That afternoon she called to thank me. That evening, I was at her apartment putting on the final touches.

Cynthia had gotten married at 18. She and her husband bore three beautiful girls. She had been married for 10 years and separated two years prior to meeting me. She said her husband had been the only man she had ever been with sexually. However, I suspect she had a brief affair with one of her husband's friends. I mean she never admitted to it but based on the things she said and the way she lit up when speaking about the dude, I imagined something went on. But it was clear she had not been with anyone sexually for quite some time.

I thought Cynthia to be naive. I mean, she would say and do things that made me wonder where she'd been all her life. She'd buy me anything she thought I needed or wanted without me saying a word. A week after I met her, she surprised me with $700 Cuban link gold chain. She bought me a half dozen outfits and gave me any amount of money I would ask for. About the third time we had sex, in the heat of passion she asked me if I loved her.

That shit caught me off guard. I stopped fucking in mid-stroke, wondering what I should say. Fuck it, I thought. I'ma do her like they did me, "Yesss Baby.... I love you," I lied. Two weeks later I moved all my shit into her apartment.

Cynthia never really talked much, except to tell me something funny someone said or did. If I asked her what she thought about a thing, she would never directly give me an answer. It appeared she would kind of wait to get an idea of what I thought about the thing and then respond very briefly in a way which reflected my thinking. She also rarely looked at me directly. I mean every time she talked to me, she'd be looking in the opposite direction. I once asked her why she wouldn't look at me. Her complexion turned reddish purple. I couldn't quite figure it out, so I let it go.

After about two months in I grew uninterested in the situation. I didn't know why. I guess I began to feel bad about how I treated her. I pretty much came and went as I pleased, did whatever I wanted to do to her sexually, and pretty much spent her checks as if they were mine. Yet, she did not complain one bit. But still, I felt I needed to go.

So, I came in one night and started an argument to give myself an excuse to pack my things and go. I was blown away when Cynthia stood in front of the door (posted) and began to beg me not to leave. She asked me what she had done wrong, and she promised not to ever do it again. She was crying snots and booggers, pleading and begging. This fucked me up. I mean, I expected some sort of pushback, but this was absolutely unexpected. So, I slowly moved closer to her, gently grabbed a handful of her hair, and kissed her mouth softly. Then I kissed her cheek, chin, nose, and forehead as I reached down in my pants to pull out my dick. She massaged it softly before getting down on her knees to suck my dick like it were a caramel-covered Popsicle.

It was the most heartfelt, passionate, intense head job she had ever given me. She stood up, smiling, kissed the side of my face and whispered, "I'm glad you're not leaving me." I held her face in my hands, kissed her mouth and said, "I'm still leaving."

Cynthia stood there with her mouth open, crying, eyes wide with disbelief. She began to threaten to kill herself with a handful of pills if I left. I left anyway.

Three hours later doctors from General Hospital were calling my Mom's apartment asking for me to come to the hospital because Cynthia had OD'd and wanted to see me. I thought, "This Bitch is crazy." Had it not been for my Mom telling me to go see her, I never would have gone. The doctors asked me if she had ever tried anything like this before. I told them I had not known her for that long. The doctor said her stomach was pumped of the pills she swallowed. He said if she had waited a little longer to get to the hospital she may have suffered more serious issues. I went in to see her. She lay there in the bed looking like an abandoned puppy. Out of pity, and the thought of continuing to use her, I moved back in.

CHAPTER 12

Ain't nothing like it

Henry Street, where Cynthia lived, was a popular drug area. I blended in perfectly. I began selling crack all day and sniffed coke all night. One night an older familiar looking woman approached. "Hey Honey, you ain't never had your dick sucked like I'll suck it. I know you like that dick sucked, I heard about you. Come on, give me two caps, and I'll suck your dick like a fucken porn star." A closer look at the woman revealed that I did know her. She was Todd's mother! "Nah, nah, that's okay, I'm cool." "Come on now Honey, I know you want that thing buffed," she said, using the terminology young people used for head and reaching for my pants. "Go 'head man," I said, "I ain't doing nothing, go ahead!" I said, angrily. I walked away from her. "Fuck you then."

I thought about Todd's mother all night, wondering how she could allow herself to get as messed up on that shit as she did. Her son was a drug dealer, too. I wondered how he felt about his Mom going around offering to suck the dick of the people he hustled with every day. Young people half her age. I thought to myself. "Crack is a bad muthafucka." "Let me get seven for $50," the young, pregnant girl interrupted my thoughts. "Here you go Baby."

I got home about 4 a.m. and sat at the table to count my money and product. Still thinking how powerful crack must be. I held a cap in between my thumb and forefinger, looking at it, turning it over as if to find something out about it. I had seen the way crackheads made homemade pipes out of soda or beer cans by poking holes in the side of the can with a safety pin; then they'd sprinkle cigarette ashes over them, which acted as a screen. They'd put the rock atop the ashes, put their mouth to the original hole in the can, then apply a match or lighter to the rock of crack as they inhaled.

I got up from the table, went to the garbage and found a Pepsi can. I thought to myself, "I gotta see what this shit is all about." I filled my lungs with the smoke and held it for three seconds. When I exhaled, my dick instantly became rock hard. Sweat poured from my forehead. My eyes grew to the size of silver dollars and my heart seemed to be beating a thousand miles a minute. I'd never experienced anything like this. The feeling is similar to sniffing coke; but magnified X 20. I was fucked up. By the time I got up from the table I had smoked every cap I had.

Everything was cool for a while. I managed to still sell and smoke crack, on the low, of course; because crackheads were considered the lowest form of human life. I still went out to the Shangri-La to hang out with Kas and Trick, or hang out on Monroe Street, or hang out with the other crack dealers. I even went with Cynthia to shows and movies and stuff until crack took complete hold of my life.

I began losing enormous amounts of weight because crack suppressed my appetite for food. I got much darker in the face. I wasn't concerned anymore about my appearance; and that fiery, confident and fearless personality had become just a memory.

Cynthia would give me her whole paycheck to get more product to make money, but it never worked. I'd buy an ounce and a half of crack in NY, but by the time I got back to Jersey, I'd have maybe a half ounce left. Cynthia asked me on several occasions if I smoked crack because she'd heard it on the street. I'd deny it, then go into the bathroom with my homemade pipe and smoke two or three caps before heading out to the block.

I must admit, the sex was outstanding. I had molded her to do any and everything I liked. And, because she loved me so much, she perfected everything. She stood about 5' 10" and weighed in at about 250 pounds. But she worked her body like 120 pound, 21-year-old college girl. However, crack and dope satisfied me more.

Sex with Cynthia eventually became non-existent, and the drugs had demolished any desire for it. When I did call myself having sex with her it lasted two minutes. Literally. I'd cum one time and didn't even think about her not being satisfied. I only thought about that crack and went into the bathroom to smoke it every time we finished. After a while Cynthia lost all respect for me. She talked to me any way she wanted to, which would usually be cold and callous.

She had no problem with finding herself two or three other guys to pick up the slack, while I was out doing my thing. Although I really couldn't have cared less about her episodes. She made no attempt, or very subtle ones, at trying to hide them. I used to ask her about some of her episodes just to see what she'd say. She would lie, and suggest the crack was making me paranoid.

Cynthia had taken up with an ex-athlete-turned playboy drug dealer named Tank. She kind of kept it on the low, but eventually it became obvious that she couldn't have cared less. Cynthia contracted a venereal disease from Tank, which she then gave me. By the time I realized something was wrong with my dick, (before I figured out that she had burned me, rather than me burning her) she had given me penicillin pills to give to Tank. He had asked her if she had any antibiotics lying around that he could have. I guess she figured I'd take some too, which I did. I didn't say anything to her or him about it because I didn't want to create any drama in our unspoken arrangement.

Actually, it mattered a damn to me what she did. As long as she kept giving me that paycheck every week to buy my crack, she could have burned me on a weekly basis; I didn't give a damn. In fact, she did burn me once more, and we went through the same routine. They must have thought I was crazy as hell not to question what they were doing. I was. I was crazy about that crack.

She also took up with a fellow crackhead, which puzzled me. I thought I was too much for anybody to put up with, considering the hours I kept and the money of hers that I spent. But she managed it. I had heard about the relationship between Cynthia and "Robert," as she called him, on the street a few times, but I didn't believe it. I didn't believe it because she struck me as selective, and not the kind of woman who would give up the pussy to just anybody. Especially not BigHead Bobby.

One night I came home a bit earlier than usual, and to my surprise, the chain lock was on the door. When she finally unlocked the door and let me in, I went into the bedroom. I immediately smelled what I believed to be stinking feet and ass. I imagined she had just finished doing her thing with "whoever" and probably had sent them home minutes before I had arrived. But what had actually happened was, Cynthia and BigHead Bobby had been caught in the act! When I knocked on the door, she had hidden him in the kids' room in their closet (they weren't home) until I fell asleep. Then, in the kid's room, finished what they had started in her bedroom.

That incident fucked me up, because he broadcasted this information on the block in detail, including how he had butt-fucked her. It further fucked me up because she was now showing that she had no respect for herself. I mean, I wasn't respectworthy; but to allow this ugly, dirty crackhead to come into her house, fuck her in the ass, then hide him in her kids' closet... The kids found a crusty, dirty sock in the closet weeks later. They brought the sock to the bedroom where she and I were to show her. She told her kids the sock was: "What we gone call a skeleton in the closet." Right in front of me. Bitch!!

I was tempted to whoop BigHead Bobby's ass on several occasions, but my weight was way below normal, and my heart (courage) was gone long before this incident. There wasn't an ounce of fight left in me. Actually, I did confront him and asked why he put his business out in the street like that. His response was that she had been sweating him and he wanted it to be known. Translation: "Fuck You!!!"

I knew that he wanted me to leave her so that he could step in. However, that wasn't gonna happen. But I made a mental note that, if I ever returned to the real Raheem, the first ass that I was gonna whoop would be his, and he knew it. I was gonna whoop his ass not for fucking Cynthia, because she allowed it to happen, but because he put it out there on the street, embarrassing me beyond belief.

I asked about the situation just to see what her response would be, and again, she denied it strongly. Well, not just denied it, but swore on her kids and her Mom that it was all untrue. That's when I knew that she should have been an actress. I mean, she acted as if I actually didn't know any better, and that I MUST believe she was telling the truth.

Over the next two years Cynthia fucked Chuck, the main guy I was hustling with; Box; BigHead Bobby; her husband; her husband's best friend; a younger guy she worked with at Macy's while she worked there part time; and even Teddy, the guy who cut me.

If I'd ever had any, I had lost any respect I had for her. I didn't understand why she allowed me to stay at her apartment, give me her weekly check, bail me out of jail countless times, took my verbal abuse, yet give herself away so easily to so many different guys. I knew I wasn't doing my job in the bedroom, or any other room for that matter. But if she wanted to just give the pussy away to anybody who asked for some, why didn't she just say that and send me on my way, rather than let me and everybody else use her like that. I figured it was just the foul shit women did.

I mean, I didn't love her, I only used and grew dependent upon her; and I believe she knew it, but didn't care. I further believe that because of her being married at such a young age for so long, she never really got a chance to do the things and experience the people a person who wasn't married with children would normally experience.

When I met her, my lifestyle and popularity thrust her into the spotlight. She became a brand-new person, trying to make up for lost time, not realizing that she was losing all of who she was as a result. I don't think she realized that after I was done with her, that no decent person who knew me, or who was about anything positive would want her. She was considered weak, gullible, easy and the worst kind of liar: one who didn't have to lie but lied anyway. But I was in no position to tell her that. I was a crackhead trying to get all I could get from her.

The events in my life were indicative of the drugs I used, and the neglect and trauma I had endured; all of which had molded me into the person I had become. No one had ever told me or showed me the difference between right and wrong, and although I believe there is an innate internal meter of what is right and wrong, I developed my own warped, sick, dysfunctional value system, which included that if I did wrong long enough, it would start to feel right.

No one ever really disciplined me, other than the law; but they had to catch me first, and even then, it didn't compare to the instant gratification I got by doing wrong. Especially if I got away with it. So, I ended up always taking chances.

No one had ever taken the time to talk to me, to explain the real facts of life, like the importance of an education, family, hard work, patience. No one explained the dangers of procrastination, lies, crime and drugs. So, as a result, I escaped reality through drugs.

No one ever taught me about love in general or told me how important it is to have love in one's life; so, I never understood or knew how to love. If ever I acquired a strong attachment to anyone, I'd quickly distance myself from them.

Outside of my Mom, Grandma and sisters, I had never met a woman who wasn't either weak, disloyal, gullible, a sex fiend, a liar, gullible, or desperate. So, I never really respected women. I'd always be outwardly cordial and polite, but in my heart of hearts, I harbored some of the vilest thoughts possible about them.

CHAPTER 13

The most valuable experience

The legal process of the whole robbery ordeal was painfully slow. I plead guilty to robbery. I was caught red-handed, so there was no need for a trial. Eleven months passed before I was finally sentenced to 15 years, with a mandatory minimum of four years.

It was especially painful because I had to kick two habits: an insatiable crack/cocaine (psychological) habit and a monster dope (physical) habit. Going through the physical withdrawals from the dope was hell: vomiting every 20 minutes, hot and cold flashes, migraine headaches, backaches and constant diarrhea. But the psychological withdrawal from the crack was twice as painful. Everything I saw looked like a rock of crack. I thought "crack" daily: smelled it in the air, tasted it in everything I ate, and I even dreamed about it every night. I am convinced that crack is the most powerful drug in the world.

When I finally reached Rahway State Prison I was as scared as a lamb in a lion's den. I had attended a program called Scared Straight when I was 10 years old; which basically was a program where teachers, Boys

Club counselors, Elders of churches, social workers and juvenile detention centers would get the "problem kids," and take them to Rahway State Prison: to get the piss literally scared out of them.

The children would be ushered into the prison's auditorium and instructed to sit down on hard wood seats and bleachers and be quiet while a dozen men serving life sentences, for crimes ranging from murder to robbery, stood just inches away from their faces and verbally abused them.

All of these men, on the day that I attended, were extremely intimidating, physically and verbally. Their average weight was at least 250 pounds, their faces reflected their anger and pain as they yelled at us, calling us "little Bitches" and "Fags." One guy, who I remember as Patch Eye, said that he'd be the first to fuck any of us if we ever stepped foot in that prison to do time.

He was only about 5'5" but he weighed at least 250 pounds, all muscle. What was particularly scary about Patch Eye was the expression on his face. His mouth seemed to be stuck in position to utter only the word: "muthafucka." He only had one eye, which was extremely red. He wore a patch where the other one used to be. He said he lost his eye on a bet, so he pulled it out of his head himself and gave it to the guy he lost the bet to, which was probably bullshit, but at the time, whatever he said was the Gospel truth.

The men displayed broken paint rollers on tables which were straightened out and sharpened, to be used as daggers; as well as other hideous homemade knives that looked like they'd kill someone instantly.

We were completely horrified. In fact, one girl urinated on herself when Patch Eye got right up in her face and told the girl that he'd liked to fuck her in her eye socket.

All the memories came rushing back and shaped the first two days of my stay. After being issued State clothing, I was housed in 4 Wing, which instantly reminded me of The House That Jack Built. A four level, eight-tier building, painted a dreary, clay-color gray. The only obvious difference was that there was always someone there. There were 46 cells on either side of the wing, mine was number 36, Left Wing, 8 Tier. As I walked down the tier quickly, I noticed, in my peripheral vision, how different cells were in terms of cleanliness. Some cells looked as if you could eat off the floor, while others looked and smelled like gas station restrooms.

My cell was a bare, dusty, 6'x9', vomit-green color; with a six-foot long bed that folded against the wall. The toilet and sink (one piece) and a board were attached to the steel wall, which was used to shelve a TV.

It was about 7:00 p.m. I had obviously missed dinner. I pulled down the bed and laid on it, watching the roaches play tag on the ceiling. I lay there awake, thoughtless, afraid to think of what the next day would bring. Then, suddenly, out of the darkness, "psss, psss, yo, yo, what's your name man?" Scared to death, but conscious of where I was, I said, "Why, and who the fuck are you?" "Don't talk so loud man, my name is Dean. I just came down to see if you need anything, you all right?" "I don't know you," I said. "Yeah, I'm all right." He paused for a second and then said, in that distinctive homosexual manner, "You want some work?"

"Get the fuck away from my door," I yelled angrily. "C.O. yo, yo C.O. Come get this muthafucka!"

Unaffected by my reaction, he simply sucked his teeth, rolled his eyes and walked away. The guy next door in 37 cell yelled over. "Yo, 36, was that Dean?" I didn't respond. 37 laughingly said, "Yo, that fag-ass joker is always floating around here four and five in the morning looking for a dick to suck. Next time throw some piss in his face."

I didn't know what to make of what had just happened, I only knew I was a little more afraid than I had been a few minutes ago. So, I turned on the light and laid there awake until breakfast.

"4 Wing, Tiers 6 and 8, mess out!! Wings 6 and 8, mess out," the lady bellowed over the PA system. The cell bars opened. I was hungry as hell. The door sprung open. I nervously exited my cell onto the tier and just followed the crowds, praying that I didn't run into a '90s version of Patch Eye.

As soon as I walked into the mess hall there was a sea of faces that I recognized, and even knew, from my hometown of Passaic. "Raheem, what's up man?!" a voice excitingly inquired. I slowly turned around, hoping that this wasn't the voice of someone I had robbed before, and said, without expression, very seriously, "I'm all right." "Yo, man, it's me Nah, Nasim from Paterson." "Oh shit," I muttered, half embarrassed, half surprised.

"What's up soldier?" extending my hand. "How have you been man?" "I'm all right, what the fuck are you doing here?" Robbery, 15 with 7 1/2," I lied. "What wing you on? You need anything?" Nasim asked sincerely. "Nah, I'm cool. I'll be all right once my people send my gear," I said. "Okay, well dig man, I'll see you in the yard, let me get something to eat." "All right, peace," I said extending my hand again.

I shook a few more hands and nodded at a few more guys that I knew, but I was especially glad to see Nasim. I met him 10 years prior at a youth correctional institution called Jamesburg. He was the most fearless short Nigga I had ever met. He was definitely among the best fighters in our Jamesburg days. I had also gone to see him in Paterson when he got out. He was even more dangerous. He'd bust a joker in the head with a golf club or stab a joker to death in a New York minute.

I remembered once while visiting Nasim, it had gotten back to Nasim that the next-door neighbor had stolen his sister's TV. Nasim and I wanted the guy to come outside so that we could confront him. But as soon as he realized we were waiting for him, he started to run. We caught him and commenced to whooping his ass, no mercy. He managed to get away for a minute and get into his parents' house. Nasim kicked the door down, grabbed a bat which was near the door, and beat the neighbor into a coma. He was also here in Rahway for robbery. Nasim was definitely a person I was glad to know.

The yard reminded me of Harlem's 125th Street on a Saturday night. Most everyone wore the latest style of clothes, jewelry and sneakers. People were selling dope, coke, crack, weed, and pills. They were gambling and even robbing people. The only thing the yard lacked were women, well, real women. Boy pussy was available for those who were so inclined.

I walked through the yard practically in a daze, overwhelmed by the fact that so much was going on in a place that I thought was supposed to be like a P.O.W. Prison Camp. Yet, in addition to those activities, guys played full court basketball, baseball, handball, soccer and even bocce ball. This place was not even close to the hell I had imagined it could be, at least not yet.

"Yo, Rah, what up fam?" Nasim shouted from the poker table and motioned me over. "What's up man? You winning?" I asked, nonchalantly, not wanting him to notice my amazement. "I'm doing all right. Hold up," he said, as he dealt the last card of "7 Cards All Down." He dealt himself a nine of spades which gave him a straight, the winning hand. "I'm out." Nasim grinned as he counted up his chips. The house man recounted and then gave Nasim 36 packs of assorted cigarettes.

We walked around the track a few times, talking about the old days, before Nasim called out to Ali. "Yo, what's up soldier? You got that?" Nasim inquired. "Yeah, what you want now?" Ali replied. Give me two bags for $30, and I'll hit you off with the other $10 on visit day," Nasim said. "All right, here." Ali gave him two bags of heroin, with the words "Blue Thunder" printed on the bag. "See you Saturday," Ali said, looking Nasim directly in the eyes without expression. "Right?" "Yeah, Saturday," said Nasim, simultaneously walking away.

After checking to see which bag was bigger, Nasim gave me the smaller of the two and said, "just give it back when you get it." The dope was good! The effects of it had me scratching constantly, my mouth was as dry as cotton, and I spoke to everyone I passed. Nasim had drifted off to sit on the benches so that he could nod.

I ended up talking to a white guy by the baseball field I thought I knew. I didn't know him, but we talked about everything under the sun. He was high, too. His name was Rocco, a tall biker-type dude. It seemed that no matter what Rocco and I talked about he always interjected an element of violence. For example: he was telling me how easy it was to have sex with one of the female guards; but halfway through his thoughts he said things like, "Yeah, but I'd like to slice one of their fucken throats, man, you know what I mean? And watch them fucken gasp for air while they fucken look at me in disbelief. You know what I mean?" Ordinarily I would have said, "Yeah, I know what you mean man. Hey listen, I got to go take care of a few things, I'll see you later," and stay as far away as I could from this maniac, but at this point I was grooving, so I said, "Yeah, man, I can dig it, by the way, where can I get me a nice piece to keep up in my cell? Just in case I got to stick something in a muthafucka." "Oh man, I got plenty of fucken shanks," he offered. "What Wing you on?" "4 Wing, 8 Tier, 36 Cell," I said. "All right, cool man, I'm in 1 Cell, I'll bring something down and let you check it out.

That was too quick and easy I thought; besides, I didn't have any money. So, I told him to hold on to it until I got my funds together. "Don't worry about it," he agreed. "Just straighten me out when you get it, we're on the same tier, don't worry about it." Against my better judgment. "Fuck it," I thought, "See you when we get inside."

"Inmate Akmadir-Nahsif #233586 report back to your wing immediately!" bellowed the PA system. I had just sat down at the table in the Mess Hall to eat. The dope was wearing off and my stomach was growling. Inmate Akmadir-Nahsif #233586 report to your wing immediately!" the voice bellowed with urgency over the PA system. Nasim looked over his shoulder at me and said, half-jokingly, "Ain't that you Rah? You better go see what's happening man, before they come and get you."

After emptying my tray, I walked to the wing trying to figure out what was so urgent that it would require them to page me. But as soon as I reached 8 Tier I was quickly informed. I was told to turn around and put my hands behind my back. It seemed like everyone was out of their cells to see what was going on. "For what?" I asked. "For possessing a weapon. Now turn the fuck around!" yelled the sergeant. The biker guy had set me up, the muthafucka!!!

I was angry as hell, but this was also an opportunity to make an impression on the inmates that were watching. "Get the fuck outta here. I don't got no fucken weapon," I spat. "All right let's go asshole," the sergeant said as about 10 guards descended upon me, twisting my arms. I cursed, spat foul names in their faces, all the way to lock up, where they all got a few punches off. Not too bad, I thought, considering all the shit I was talking.

I was given disciplinary charges and sanctions to serve 180 days in Administrative Segregation. Within my first two days, I had sniffed the best dope I'd ever had; been set up; and was in lock-up. All of which set the tone for my next 12 1/2 years of incarceration at Rahway State Prison.

The guards, whether they had been involved in the prior incident or not, treated me like shit every chance they got. They wrote me up on disciplinary charges or harassed me, which kind of forced me to uphold the first impression I had projected. So, when they harassed me, or wrote me up, I'd talk slick and say stupid shit that I would immediately regret. Needless to say, Administrative Segregation was my prison away from prison. Actually, throughout my stay at Rahway, I had been in Administrative Segregation seven times. 180 days each stay.

Come to find out, the biker dude hadn't set me up. Snowball (A long-time prisoner/gay dude) reported the guards found the shank when they performed a random search. They had searched five cells simultaneously. I had placed the knife in my boot, thinking that it was a secure place to hide it. Obviously, it was not.

During my stay at Rahway, I managed to become addicted to heroin again and picked up a gambling habit. Negativity seemed to have always swallowed me up. I did nothing but get high and gamble all day. However, when I got locked up in Ad Seg I would work out like a beast to pass the time.

When Cynthia visited me at the prison, she used to look at me with such contempt; because I would always tell her to bring me money when she came to visit. And, as soon as she'd bring me $100, I'd have my hand out for another one; and despite her contempt, if she had money and I asked for it, she'd give it to me. I'm sure she knew what I was doing with the money, because I had taken her through this same ritual on the streets. But I didn't give a fuck. I was draining her dry.

I never understood why she put up with all that. When she visited, I'd get the money first, have sex with her in the Visit Hall, or let her give me head until I came. Then I'd spend the majority of the of the visit time walking around the Visit Hall trying to find out who had dope. Cynthia just sat there looking around as if she didn't give a damn what I did. I never understood her. At times she claimed and acted as if she loved me, yet at other times she acted like a 35-year-old whore who didn't have a care in the world.

Loyalty, the true sense of the word, I imagined, was definitely not one of her better qualities, considering all the guys she fucked during our short arrangement, yet she continued to take care of me while I was in Rahway.

Clothes, food, money, and even drugs. I never understood her.

During my stay at Rahway, she had even taken up with her best friend's man, moved him into her home, and bailed him out of jail when he got busted for selling drugs, all the while continuing to profess her undying love for me. She was strange, and I appreciated her, but because of her vile actions I could never trust her or respect her. Not to mention, I could not ever believe one word she spoke.

One occasion while in Ad-Seg, a guy named JR had recently come on the tier and was put in the cell next to me. When other prisons' lock-ups got filled they would send some of their prisoners to Rahway Ad-Seg. When I learned he was from Paterson, we talked all the time through the vents. We got on the subject of people we may have commonly known. He began to talk about some fat Bitch from Passaic named Cynthia. He showed me a letter from Cynthia asking, among other things, for him to put her name on his visiting list, so she could come visit him, because she needed to hear his voice up close. "It always sounded so sexy," she had written to him. "Yeah, I know the Bitch." I admitted. I spared him the details.

I had never been so humiliated in all my life. I mean here I was in prison, supposedly in a relationship with this strange, foul woman who everybody knew was my woman, and she does this shit?!?! I was beyond words to express how I felt. She visited me every Visit Day, and despite her underhandedness, had stood by me for years. Yet, in this letter, she was practically begging to come to see this guy in the same prison with me, who's locked up next door to me, who looked like the frog from Courageous Cat and Minute Mouse!!!! I couldn't believe it. I was hurt and embarrassed.

I later found out that the guy wasn't the first guy she had written. She was writing to some other guy who had also been in the prison, but had since gone home; and another guy in Northern State Prison. I wanted to kill her. To pour gas on her and set her fat ass on fire. Instead, I vowed to hate her and never trust women for as far as I could I throw them. The ordeal with Cynthia and all the other women in my life completely destroyed not only my faith in women, but in people.

I became very bitter and kind of a garbage head over the years. However, I really only associated with a select few, mostly older, drug-dealer guys, and others who had something constructive on their minds. Homer Johnson, my homie, was someone I liked to talk to. He was a very serious, yet violent, individual who always had something profound to say. He, probably unknowingly, taught me a lot about other people as well as about myself.

I had been disciplinary-free for about six months and was given the privilege of living in the dormitories. I hated it. But I lived with it, because I had to if I didn't want to go back to AdSeg.

Homer and I slept across from each other. One night I had been stressing over the latest gossip which was about Cynthia. She had been having a sexual field day with some dude who was in the Camp section of the prison. From what I heard, he was a young Jamaican dude. I don't know why it stressed me. I knew the kind of freak she was, but still I had been stressing, asking myself how could she do the things she did to people with a clear conscience?

Homer finally came over to my bed area and sat on the footlocker. "You alright over here Player?" he said facetiously. "I'm cool," I said flatly, as if I weren't bothered by the form of his question.

"Come on brother, I heard about Cynthia and her new flavor of the day. Man, listen," he said, almost in frustration, "Every other week you sit up in that bed like a wounded cat, worried about what that girl's doing. Man, just like the homosexual say that they're the way they are from birth, just like the rapist rationalizes that they can't enjoy sex unless they take it, and just like kleptomaniacs claim they can't resist stealing; this is the way Cynthia is. Her actions simply define who she is. What she does ain't no personal reflection of who you are. She would be doing the same shit even if she was with a millionaire or political figure. She may put a little more shade on it, but she would continue to do it. Yo man, she's simply doing what she enjoys doing. So, leave that shit alone and move on man." He was right. I was letting her disturb my groove. I thought about that all night. She was disturbing my groove.

Cynthia came to visit on that Saturday. She looked a bit nervous when she sat down. "You good? I inquired. "Yes, I'm good, but I got something I want to tell you." Looking at the ground she spoke softly. "I let Earl move in with me," she announced. "What, Why? What you talking about?!" "Yeah, he been aiming at me for a while, so yes, we together," she said, almost pridefully. "Ain't that your best friend Linda's man? And don't she got AIDS?" I questioned angrily. "Yeah, but he don't got it. Besides, we used condoms," she spat. I looked at her like she had lost her mind. In fact, I was so disgusted with her, I simply walked away from her.... After she gave me the hundred dollars I had asked her to bring.

That was the last time she visited me. I put in a slip to see the doctor next doctor call to take an AIDS test. I was excited and a bit surprised that I did not have it, because on every visit Cynthia and I had, we fucked and sucked as if we were a bedroom.

For the next few years, I had a slew of woman visit me. I had reached out to a few women I had known prior to me coming to prison and, while out on visit, I made it my business to introduce myself to guys who appeared to have a large presence of female visitors. So, I usually had a visitor every Visit Day. Which meant I always had money, sex, and drugs.

CHAPTER 14

"The Champ"

Homer and I talked until 4:00 in the morning about some people we both knew on the streets. He mentioned Nola, an older woman whose family was prominent in Passaic where we're from. Everyone knew Nola, not only because of her family's status but because she was cool. She was always cordial. She hung out at the local clubs, got high from time to time, and she kept herself a younger man. She was 52, about 5'5", 300 pounds, and average looking in the face. But I think what made her attractive to most of the younger guys was her family's loot; and from what I understood, she didn't mind paying for a young man's time, for an older guy's time either. We had a good laugh about Nola, "The Champ," as Homer had nicknamed her, for whatever reason.

She and I were friendly. I had done some business with her family and on several occasions, I had even asked her out to lunch but she never accepted. One day, out of boredom, I called Nola's job to say hello, and to get the lowdown on what was happening out on the streets. She was a bit surprised to hear from me, but we laughed and talked for what seemed like hours: about her, how things were going with me, and about life in general.

I'd never had a conversation like the one I had with Nola. The conversation seemed to be a sincere and honest one, with no strings attached. I even asked her about the rumors that she paid to be with younger men. Her response was that she was somewhat financially stable and could afford to go out and spend money on the things she liked to do; and if the person she's hanging out with, male or female, that night can't afford to do things she likes to do, then she didn't mind helping the person out. She said she knew about the rumors and could care less about what people said. She went on to say that yes, she likes younger men, and if the illusion of getting her money attracts young, or younger, men, she didn't mind. She said as long as *she* knows that they aren't really getting it. Not anything of significance, anyway. Before hanging up I asked her if it was all right for me to write to her. She said yes, I told her I would, and I did.

We wrote each other long letters each week and talked on the phone nearly every night. We listened to each other without interruption. We advised each other without judging, and we talked to each other without trying to impress. I respected her wisdom and admired her strength but because of Cynthia and most every other woman I had known, I expected bullshit to show up somewhere down the line.

Nola appeared to be different from any woman I'd ever met. Actually, it was only due to her wisdom and what appeared to be sincere concern for me that I began to look deep within my own self to find out who I really was. In fact, she had asked me that once: "Who are you?" she had asked pensively. That question kind of took me by surprise, so I simply said, "I'm Raheem, are you all right?" I asked, not understanding her reasoning for the question. "No, I know your name, silly," she said lightheartedly. "I mean, who are you, as a person?" I was silent, lost in thought. "Raheem," she said seriously, "Everyone should find out who they are, what they are made of. If they don't, their happiness is lost, and they'll never know where to look in order to find it."

Profound is an understatement, I thought! I pondered that question for years before I ever attempted to answer it, even if only to myself.

CHAPTER 15

Looking for some answers

First call Jumah prayer coming out of all wings. Jumah prayer coming out of all wings," the officer announced. I had always been interested in Islam, especially when I was younger. I had even adopted the name Raheem when I learned what it meant (Merciful, Compassionate.) The Black Muslims back in the day, professed the black man should be drug-free, independent, and own their own business. They should raise their families and avoid anything that is not upstanding and just. The message appealed to me, but I thought it unrealistic. So, I never really took time out to understand the magnitude of what this religion represented. I thought a person simply adopted an Arabic name, eliminated pork, and believed in Allah for them to become Muslim.

When I walked into the small classroom, which doubled as a Masjid on Fridays, I was immediately impressed by so many men, so-called criminals, of all races, coming together and physically embracing one another with smiles on their faces and obvious love in their hearts; greeting each other with sincere.

As-salamu-alaikum. (Peace be unto you.) Their faces were so radiant; their dress modest, but immaculate; and the pleasurable scent of sandalwood and musk oils that they wore enveloping the room.

A man, the Imam, stood behind the podium in the left corner of the room, the only piece of furniture in the room, as the believers sat on the blanket-covered floor, in perfectly straight and spaced rows. As a guest, I sat off to the side, not wanting to be in the way, content and proud to just be among so many disciplined and God-fearing men. I knew that this was where I wanted to be.

The Iman, a short, slim, almost fragile man, began to speak and everyone listened intently. He spoke in Arabic first, and then translated what he said into English: "The name of God most gracious, most merciful, I bear witness that there is no God except Allah; and I bear witness that Muhammad of over 1,460 years ago is the messenger and final messenger of Allah. For those who follow God, no one can lead him astray; and *for those who God allows to be led astray, no one can lead them to righteousness; for God has power over all things.*"

The Imam spoke so eloquently and clearly. I was captivated by every word, but for some reason the words: *"for those who God allows to be led astray, no one can lead them to righteousness; for God has power over all things,"* stuck in my mind all night long.

I came back each Friday for prayer classes, Quran reading, and Arabic classes. Finally, I took Shahada, declaring myself Muslim in front of the Muslim community.

My life was changing, I thought. I began attending mosque, and I hadn't been high in five months, which was amazing for me. I remember thinking on a whole other level. I couldn't remember ever going two weeks without getting high. I had begun working out, continued not eating pork (I had stopped long ago), and began reading Islamic material regularly. I even tried to give up smoking, but it didn't work. However, I felt like I was becoming a new person.

Nola sent me a book on how to start a business. I read it cover to cover four times, took notes, and even had Nola call banks and other agencies; to gather information that I might need when I got home and attempted to make some good of myself. I had never known what hard work would bring, but I was willing to try it. I figured anything would be better than the 32 years I had already lived.

The next six years went by slowly. I gave everything I had to becoming the guy I thought I wanted to be: an upstanding, drug-free, independent, and God-fearing dude. And, with Nola's help, I had even managed to pay off the fines I owed to the Violent Crime Association.

CHAPTER 16

The Come Up

I had $1,000 saved up in my account. This was the beginning of what I believed to be the point where I lost focus. All that money in my account, seeing all my friends playing poker, getting high as hell every visit, and talking slick in the yard appealed more to me. It was what I wanted to be doing, I thought. "Maybe I can find a balance," I reasoned.

I began to do drugs again. Because I felt like it would make me forget about all of the things that had been going on with Cynthia and myself. It wasn't long before I acquired a beast of a habit. So much so that when I woke up in the morning, I had to have a bag of dope right then right there in order to function for the day.

One evening I went over to 2 Wing to buy a bag of dope to have on deck for the morning wake up. When I was exiting the wing one of the officers asked me what I was doing in that area. I told him that I was just dropping off a couple of packs of cigarettes to my nephew who had just come into the prison that week. This officer had nothing else better to do, and decided he wanted to search me. He actually found the two bags of dope that were in the watch pocket of my jeans. His face became filled with glee as if he had made the biggest drug bust in America. I laughed as he escorted me straight over to 1 Left, which was lockup. However, inwardly, I screamed, "Damn!!"

My homie, Alameen had suggested long ago that if I ever got into one of these fixes that I should always have an ugly big shank buried in the yard. The plan was to tell the officer that I knew where a shank was, and that I had overheard "someone" plotting to stab "someone" the next day in the yard. I'd tell the officer where the shank was if he let me go. I had used this ruse before. So, I knew it worked. All they wanted was to get their hands on the shank. They really didn't give too much of a damn who put it there, they just wanted it to ensure their asses didn't get poked up. However, this time I had forgotten to take the suggestion.

I kicked myself in the ass all night. I silently prayed that someone would walk through, so that I could send a message to Lenny Munn, 6 Fingers, or Nasim, but that prayer was never answered.

As I laid in my bunk that evening, sleep evading me, I listened to two guys on the upper tier (which was not lock-up) having a disagreement about some dumb shit. One dude began threatening the other: "muthafucka, when the doors bust in the morning you better have your fucken boots laced up real tight because I'm coming up in there to do you real dirty, Nigga. You soft ass muthafucka," he spat venomously. The other dude (the soft ass muthafucka) did not respond. He said absolutely nothing. When the doors opened the following morning, the guy who threatened to "do the soft-ass muthafucka" dirty was still asleep. However, the "soft ass muthafucka" was wide awake and (from what I heard) entered the dude's cell, straddled the dude's back as he slept, and sank a rusty shank into the dude's back and head over 30 times. It was ugly.

Ultimately, I ended up in Administration Segregation for another six months stay. I had been there so many times that I had no more good time for the administration to take, so I would end up maxing out from Ad Seg.

As it got closer and closer to my release date, I remember being more and more afraid. I was afraid because I only had the experience of leaving a prison or institution and returning soon after for committing some crime. This was the cycle that I was used to. I did not know any other way to live other than being a drug addict criminal. However, this time I wanted to do something different. But I just didn't know how or believe that I could. This scared me.

Broom Hilda's words began to ring in my ears. "You ain't shit, you ain't never gonna be shit, you gonna die before you reach 18 or you gonna be in prison for the rest of your life. You dumb black muthafucka. You almost nothing." I began to cuss God, question God, as to why he had dealt me this hand. Why did he make me out to be this person: a nothing, a nobody, possibly dying having done nothing with my life.

CHAPTER 17

Big Ideas

Nola and I had become something more than friends. She had come to visit me. She genuinely cared about me and my well-being and did everything possible to help me in whatever I endeavored. I often felt guilty asking for and receiving things from her, because I knew in my heart of hearts that there could never be a long-lasting, intimate, committed love kind of relationship between Nola and me. She was now 58 years old, had a 26-year-old son, and had reached all of her life goals. I was just beginning to think about my life, so to speak. I mean, I liked her, a whole lot; but I just wasn't looking to have a long-lasting committed type of emotional, intimate relationship with her. I just hoped that we'd remain friends, because her friendship was one that I valued and respected.

June 26th, 2001, at 9:10 a.m. I was released from Ad Seg, and I stood in front of Rahway State Prison's doors waiting for Nola to pick me up. It had been 11 years nine months and 15 days since I'd been in the Free World, and I was supposed to be overwhelmed with joy. In a way, I guess I was, but I was also filled with fear of the unknown. A lot of things changed in 12 and a half years, and I didn't quite know what to expect. All I knew was my history of being released from some jail or institution and in a small matter of time going right back.

However, this bid has been the most reflective, introspective, and most valuable time in my life. It not only forced me to take a deeper look at myself, but it also helped me see people in a whole other light. The good and the bad. It taught me about truth, loyalty, respect, personal space, the importance of communication, patience and commitment.

To take my mind off my fears as I waited, I attempted to mentally answer Nola's question, "Who are you?" I was once a man who never really knew responsibility or hard work, whose morals and ethics and values never really existed. They were deeply rooted in a life of drugs and crime. I was a man who never gave anything and always wanted something.

But today I stood, a 6'3" 225-pound, bald-headed man with almost nothing; but a man realizing that at this stage in my life, my only asset was me: a man who refused to leave this life as a nobody, with nothing, and alone. I didn't know if the answer was sufficient. But it was the only one I had. The only one I rehearsed.

"Hey Honey," she said and kissed me passionately, with tears of joy rolling down her face. I caressed her soft face, and I kissed her back, and I thought of all that would follow when we got to her house. We loaded my things into her car and drove off.

I looked back at the prison and said a silent prayer for those who were still there. Nola wore a green dress, and as she drove, I caressed her legs and thighs, and I soon discovered she wore no panties. I toyed with her wet, fleshy pussy all the way to Passaic. When we arrived at her house, I did all of the things that I had told her I would, only slower and with more passion.

Nola slept. I took a shower, got dressed and used her car to go to my Mom's house. But first, I just cruised around town taking in the sights. New buildings had been erected, old ones torn down, and there were plenty of new faces, most of which seem to be expressing the effects of some sort of drug. Young girls, older women, young boys, and older men; walking around as if they were hunting something, something which sustained their very life, something so evasive yet so plentiful.

I was sincerely saddened by all of this, especially by the sight of a well-dressed young man standing on a corner arguing with an older woman. The woman turned to walk away, and the young man kicked her hard on her rear end, causing the woman to fall to the ground. He then kicked her in the face three or four times as he shouted obscenities at her.

Before I could pull the car over to help the woman off the ground, a crowd of people, men and women, had descended upon the woman like buzzards, turning every pocket she had inside out. Watching that, I grew sadder and angry, and afraid. I drove off.

"Knock, knock," "Who is it?" a voice called from inside. "Police," I said, disguising my voice. "Police? What the hell?" They opened the door. "Hey! Reesee!" my younger sisters, Teresa and Jackie, exclaimed almost simultaneously, happily embracing me. "What's up girl?" I smiled. "Hi Boy." "What's up Ma?" I muttered through the lump in my throat, as tears flooded my eyes. I hugged my Mom tightly. "I love you, Mom." "I know Boy," she said lovingly. "I know." "Would you all stop all that crying and stuff?" my oldest sister, Dee Dee, interrupted, with outstretched arms to greet me. I smiled and embraced her too. My family and I had always had a very loving relationship. No matter what mistakes any of us made we were always there emotionally to support each other.

We laughed, talked, played cards and they all filled me in with what had gone on over the years. A few people in or close to the family had passed away. "You know Cynthia has been coming around lately asking when you'll be home," my Mom said, as she got up from the table to fix me a plate of food. "Forget Cynthia," I said angrily. "She better stay as far away from me as she can, because if she says one out of the way word to me, I'll bash her horse head in." My sisters laughed, but my Mom quickly interjected, sternly, "Now Boy, you know that girl is going to say something to you, so you better control your temper. You don't want to go back to that prison again for doing something stupid." "Yeah, all right. She just better stay away from me." I mumbled. Before I said my goodbyes, I told them that I loved them and where they could reach me if they needed me.

Nola was just getting out of the tub when I got back to her house. "Is that you, Raheem?" she asked, rhetorically. "You know who it is, girl," I said, walking towards her, smiling. "You expecting another horny Superman?" "Where you been?" she managed to ask, in between my wet kisses. "By my Mom's house," I assured her, as I slipped my hand under her afghan and caressed her smooth thighs.

I awoke an hour later feeling like brand new money. I took a long warm shower and prepared myself a big breakfast: four eggs; grits; six turkey sausages; four pieces of toast; a bowl of grapefruit slices; and a tall glass of cold milk. I sat at the dining room table eating and going through the want ads. I wasn't completely sure what kind of work I was looking for because it had been so long since I worked at all, but at this point anything would suffice. I just wanted to make and save up enough money to put my cleaning business into effect. I already had the $1,000 for my savings in prison, $500 Nola had given me upon my release, and $50 my Mom had slipped me when I was leaving her house.

I had circled ads for shipping and receiving: managerial positions that were available and convenient to get to and from by bus, keeping in mind that I wouldn't always have the use of Nola's car. I knew I wasn't qualified for the jobs I had circled but I always had the ability to catch on quick. Besides, as good as I was feeling that day if they allowed me to talk for just five minutes I'd get hired. Because if I couldn't rely on anything else, I could always rely on my ability to talk someone into something that they probably wouldn't ordinarily do. With that in mind, I kissed the sleeping Nola, and I was off.

It was about 8:30 a.m. when I drove onto Route 46 West. I was looking for a place called Tempco Incorporated, in Willowbrook. I had been on this road plenty of times before, at the mall, but I wasn't having any luck finding Tempco. Frustrated, I pulled over into the mall parking lot to ask someone for directions. I hated having to ask for directions. They always seemed to act as if I were asking for a lung or something, or they ended up giving confusing directions.

So, in my attempt to avoid all of that, I ended up walking past the many people who were waiting for the buses, or waiting for the mall to open, and I walked right into the mall security person.

"Excuse me man, I'm trying to find a place called Tempco, it's somewhere around here in Willowbrook, would you know where it is?" "Tempco? No, I don't think I've heard of that," he said positively. "What you can do is, go inside to the information desk and that guy can probably help you. He knows everything." "Isn't the mall closed?" I asked, confused. "Oh, tththat's right," he stammered. "Dum-Dum," I thought. "That's alright man I'll find it."

I walked around the other side of the Macy's building and noticed a young lady using the employee's door. I tried to get her attention, but she was rushing and didn't hear me yelling to her. By the time I got to the door and opened it she was gone. In fact, I didn't see anyone. Immediately my antennas went up. That scared me, because I had been hell bent on finding a job legitimately and intended to do what was right; but now, at the first sign of the possibility of getting something for nothing, my antenna goes up. "Ain't that a bitch?" I thought.

I just kind of walked through the huge store slowly trying not to be noticed. I thought if I was noticed I would just tell whoever noticed me that I was looking for the info booth as directed by security. I was actually amazed that such a store wasn't more secure. To my right, there was the diamond center; the display cases were empty but the door to a few of them were open as if they were being prepared to be stocked. I quickly walked toward that area.

I began to think to myself "What would I take if I were to take something?" I mean, anything of any significant value would take up a lot of space. And how would it look if I were seen leaving the store with an armful of whatever? Surely all of those people standing outside would be suspicious and inform someone, the police even; and what if someone sees me getting into Nola's car and takes down the license plate? And worst of all, what if I got caught!? I'd be back in prison three days after doing nearly 12 years in prison for stealing one or two measly dollars' worth of shit. The thought of the latter sent fear all through me.

Up ahead was a door which led upstairs to the refund desk, I remembered. I thought to myself: "Money!!," and my heart began to pound again in my chest. As soon as I put one foot on the stairs, I was startled by voices and ducked back through the door. "Hey, I'm going to go down and get coffee Margo, you want any?" the first voice said. "Yeah, black and sweet, Honey." the other voice replied. "Okay, be right back," "Okay," said Margo. I heard footsteps coming down the stairs. I assumed they belonged to the first voice going to get the coffee, but I also heard more footsteps and the sound of a door closing. I was confused, but I decided to go upstairs anyway. If noticed, I would now say that I was looking for the Personnel Office to apply for a job.

When I reached the top of the stairs, I noticed that the door to the Refund Office was held open by one of those little wooden door stoppers. I peeked inside the office. I saw that no one was inside. My heart again began beating a thousand beats a minute as the adrenaline rose. I opened the door slowly and quietly as I stepped in. I immediately noticed a medium-sized safe in the middle of the room with its door ajar, so I quickly took the garbage bag out of the garbage can and headed towards it, but as soon as I reached the safe, I heard a toilet flush.

The other footsteps. I couldn't think fast enough about what to do so I eased over to the restroom door, still directly in front of it, and as soon as Margo opened the door, I hit her right square in the mouth with everything I had, knocking her out cold and disconnecting a few teeth.

I closed the door quickly and commenced to empty the safe into the garbage bag, moving over to the two drawers near the refund window, which were filled with money. I practically flew down the stairs. I can't begin to explain what I was feeling inside, except feelings of excitement nearly burst my head. I tried to exit the first door I came to but remembered that the only door that was open was the employees' door. I nearly passed out realizing that I'd have to go all the way back through the store in order to get out. I wiped the sweat from my brow and proceeded to nervously walk out.

I got to Nola's car and decided to take the scenic route back to Passaic, figuring the highway would be the first place police would look if anyone from the store had seen me get into Nola's car. I drove carefully, keeping my eyes on the rearview mirror. I felt a sense of relief when I reached Passaic, but I didn't want to stay there just in case. I parked Nola's car in front of her house, put the keys in her mailbox and hurried to the nearest bus stop.

Just as I approached the bus stop, the 190 New York bus was pulling in. I regained my composure as best I could, paid the fare, and sat at the back of the bus. It was only 10:10 a.m. so there were not many people on the bus. In fact, there were only two older women and three teenagers on the bus besides me.

After getting on the bus, I waited until the bus had been well en route to its destination before I examined the loot. There were nine big green deposit bags packed to capacity in six thick, white envelopes. I unzipped one of the big green bags first. Wrapped around the money was a long strip of paper that appeared to be from a cash register. The date on the register paper was June 29th. Evidently, I had gotten my hands on the previous day's receipts. I removed a handful of money from the bag and saw there were all denominations of bills. There had to be at least $10-$12,000 in this particular bag. Just the mere thought of what was in the others made my penis as hard as Japanese calculus. The opening of each bag and envelope seem to take me to another erotic level, and by the time I opened the last bag, I was fighting back ejaculation. I put all the money into a Dunkin' Donuts bag I found on the bus floor, and I left the envelopes! and green empty bags in the garbage bag. When I exited the bus at Port Authority, I threw the garbage bag in the garbage and proceeded down the escalator.

I stopped at the nearest phone to let Nola know her car was in front of her door and everything was all right. "Hello," she said into the receiver. "Hey, Nola, what's up?" "Oh, hi Honey, where are you?" she asked. "I'm in New York, Baby, I ran into a little drama, but.... "New York?" she interrupted. "What happened Honey?" she asked, obviously alarmed. "Calm down Baby, everything is cool. Your car is downstairs, and your keys are in your mailbox. Okay? Everything is all right." I reassured her. "I'm going to check into a hotel, and then I'll call you back to let you know where I'm staying, okay?" I said, calmly. "Raheem, what happened?" "Hey," raising my voice, "Look, are you going to be home for a while?"

"Yes," she said, sounding obviously hurt. "All right then, I'll call you back in a couple of hours, okay Baby?" "Okay," she said.

After hanging up, I headed towards the street thinking of my next move. I walked to 42nd Street and down Broadway before stopping at a luggage store to buy a duffel bag for the money and a piece of luggage so that I didn't look suspicious upon checking into a hotel. Farther down Broadway is where I decided to stay, at the Milford Plaza.

As soon as I entered the room, I emptied the bag of money onto the bed. The sight of it all in one big heap nearly took my breath away. I had never been in possession of so much money, and my mind was thinking a thousand thoughts a minute as to what to do with it all. I took off my shirt and shoes, got up on the bed, sat with my legs crossed Indian style and began to count it. 42,742.... 42,743.... 42,744.... I couldn't believe it! $42,745! I didn't know whether to laugh or cry. No, I didn't know whether to laugh or cry; sing, shout; or do the fucken electric boogaloo! I was ecstatic!

The phone rang, causing me to jump clean off the bed and sweat profusely. "Who in the hell can that be?" I thought. No one knows where I am. I picked up the phone on its 4th ring.

"Hello?" I spoke nervously. "Hello, Mr. Akmadir, welcome to the Milford Plaza, this is the Hotel Manager. Are you satisfied with your room?" "Oh, yes and thank you," I said, relieved. "Is there anything we can do for you?" "No, thank you." I replied. "Okay, if you need anything don't hesitate to inform us," the manager said. "Will do, thank you."

I sat on the edge of the bed wondering what I had resorted to in just 3 days, and how I had practically abandoned all I had found in Islam. Islam had taught me to be present, to persevere, and to do good. It had taught me to be strong, as well as kept me sane during that very trying and difficult time in my life. Yet already, I had been reduced to almost everything I had vowed to forget. With tears in my eyes, I prostrated in prayer and begged for forgiveness. I asked God to forgive me and allow me the opportunity to do something productive with this money and perhaps try to make amends for this sin; to do something good for myself and others. I needed to think.

After hiding the money, I called Nola and asked her to come to the hotel. I figured she had been there for me when I would fight my demons during my stay in prison, always helping to clear my mind and she helped me to think. I decided to work out in the hotel's gym. Working out in prison had always cleared my mind and would help me to think better until she got there.

The hotel gym was fully equipped. State of the art universal weights, free weights, aerobics classes, cardiovascular equipment: the kind of stuff you see on TV. I worked out with the universal weights, did some calisthenics and ran two miles on the treadmill, before settling into the Jacuzzi for 30 minutes.

I felt a little better now and focused on getting myself situated in regard to preparing for the start of business. I laid across the bed, exhausted by the time Nola arrived. "Hi Honey, is everything okay?" she asked timidly, as she sat down on the bed next to me. "Everything's fine, Baby," I said. "I just kind of needed to get away to straighten out some business, but everything's cool now, I'm going to be staying here for a few days." "You want me to stay with you Honey?" she offered. "Sure Sweetheart, what kind of question is that?" I asked, smiling. "Well, I didn't know, I thought maybe you would have wanted to be alone or something." "No, come here." I pulled her close to me and kissed her passionately, and whispered in her ear, "I want you to stay right here with me." Then I continued to kiss her smooth face. "Bae, you're so sweaty. What have you been doing?" she moaned, as I kissed and caressed her. "Working out down at the gym." She continued to moan as she began to kiss and lick my chest. Her thick, hot, wet tongue toyed with my nipples; her hand brushed the towel aside, taking hold of my manhood, her mouth seemed to be magnetically drawn to it.

We fucked passionately for about two hours. I was now totally strengthless. I dragged myself into the bathroom, turned on the cold water in the shower, and sat there in the tub, enjoying the feeling of the cold water against my body for a few minutes before taking a shower.

When I finished showering, I wasn't surprised to find Nola still in the bed, basically in the same position I had left her. She was obviously exhausted, too. Since I'd been home, I'd put her 58-year-old body in every position that her 5'5" 250-pound frame could fit into, and I loved every minute of it. It was clear to me that I was sexually superior to her. Shit, I had just done nearly 12 years in prison, and I was 20 years her junior, but it was also clear to me that she had the tightest, hottest, wettest pussy I'd ever had in my life. I couldn't get enough of her; I thought to myself. If she were 20 years younger, I'd probably consider trying that love thing with her. She certainly possessed all the good qualities of someone worth falling in love with; except she was too old and couldn't have kids. I covered her up with the sheet and then lay there beside her, thinking about my $12,745.

The rest of the week flew by. During the days, I did things like sight-see, shop, look up apartments in the paper and even opened a small savings account. At night, Nola and I ate at nice restaurants, saw movies, saw Broadway shows and fucked until the early morning hours.

It was 6:30 a.m. Monday morning, when I was awakened by the irritating sounds of the alarm clock Nola had set. After she got dressed, kissed me and departed, I ordered breakfast, counting my money again. Not because I thought Nola would steal some of it, but because it was an old habit.

I got dressed and took a cab to the car dealership in Englewood, New Jersey. I had never owned a near-new car before, so the thought of possibly owning one danced around in my head. And, I thought, if I did get one, I want to go top of the line. However, after thinking about more, purchasing a brand-new car would exhaust all my dough. And there were so many things I wanted to do that the idea of purchasing a new car seemed a bit stupid to me. I walked out of that dealership and into the Honda dealership a few stores down. I purchased a funky little used blue on black Honda Accord. I fondly named her The Blue Goose.

I went to the nearest post office and got a Manila envelope and four stamps. I wrapped one grand in a newspaper, put it inside the envelope, addressed it to my Mom, and mailed it off. I knew I couldn't hand my Mom a thousand dollars, then look her in the eyes and tell her I didn't steal it. She'd been worried sick about me being in prison for so long; and she was now so

117

proud of the wiser and more settled person she wanted me to be. I didn't want to ruin that image.

I waited a day or so and then called her and explained excitedly that I had won 10 grand gambling. I told her that I had mailed her some money because I didn't want to walk the street to bring it to her with so much money on me. She believed that, because she knew that I once loved to gamble. I was sure she'd give me a lecture about gambling, but that was better than her arguing that I had stolen something; especially so soon. That would truly have broken her heart.

CHAPTER 18

The Jungle

Riding through Passaic was like riding through a cemetery/dance club. One block there'd be doped out men and women with their ashy faces in a deep nod: leaning on gates, walls or sitting on cars, scratching themselves raw. On other blocks there'd be bony crackhead men and women running up and down the block with dry, ashy faces and bulging eyes, trying to get their smoke on. And in the middle of all that were the drug dealers: with their Nike sweat suits, sneakers, gold chains, diamond rings, and cellular phones; leaning against their Lexus coupes, Acuras, and Benzes, while they bobbed their heads to Jay-Z's latest cut, and counted wads of money. Most all the drug dealers were young guys, mainly kids, but none of their faces were familiar to me.

But as I turned up the Main Avenue, I did see a familiar face. Haleem Hall. He was the only drug dealer I'd ever known who never took a bust. He had been arrested several times that I remember, but he never did a bid. He was known as a smart drug dealer; never carried any drugs or sold anything from his own hand. Some folks even figured that he must be a stool pigeon, but I didn't think so. In fact, I didn't put much stock into the stool pigeon theory or how he conducted his business. My opinion was that if no one could point out anyone that says he told on them, then the person making all the accusations is the one that needs to be watched. Haleem was all right with me. I liked him because he always minded his business, and he never bragged about what he had. But what I liked most about Haleem was that he never turned his nose up at me when I was strung out. "What's up Haleem, what's good?" I asked, as I stepped from my car.

"What's up player? How you doing man?" he replied, extending his hand with a smile. "Me against the world," I replied. "Damn man, you've been gone a long time, how long has it been?" "12 and a half, man." "Damn! So, when you get out?" "About two weeks ago, I've just been on the low, trying to do my thing." "Yeah, I see you. That's good bro, you still getting high?" "Nah, man that thing ain't to be fucked with." I confessed. We laughed. "Yeah man, it's good to see you out here and sucka free" extending his hand again.

We talked and laughed for about 15 minutes, when, out of the corner of my eye, I noticed BigHead Bobby finishing some sort of transaction with a young lady. I tried not to look in his direction because already my blood was starting to boil at the very sight of him.

Haleem noticed the obvious change in my demeanor and asked, "What's up with you man?

You alright?" he inquired, concerned. "I'm good bro, I see that sucker ass Nigga over there." "Who, Bobby?" Haleem asked. "He just got out too, last month but fuck that shit; whatever the issue is, it probably ain't worth no smoke." Haleem said and continued to talk about something else.

But my mind wouldn't leave BigHead and that night nearly 13 years ago. As Bighead walked towards our direction, I silently prayed that he would just walk past, without saying a word, because although I knew the smart thing to do was to let go of what had happened years ago, I also knew in my heart of hearts that if he spoke a word to me, I'd run through him like a fucken laxative.

"What's up Raheem?" Ding ding ding ding!!!! Bells rang loudly in my ears and my head seemed as hot as burning coal. "What?" I spat venomously. "What's up man? How you doing?" BigHead said. I backed up a few steps, took off my glasses, raised my fist into fighting position, and started towards him. "What's up muthafucka? You want some work?" "No, man, go ahead with that bullshit," he said as he backed up.

"No, fuck that, coward, put your shit up." I said angrily excited. "All right, fuck it, you want to fight, Nigga?" he said, as he swung at my head. I ducked and caught him with a bolo right between the eyes, knocking him back. But, as a half-ass boxer, he knew how to take a punch and keep coming. As he lurched forward, I hit him again with three solid punches square in the mouth. He spat out a few teeth and rushed me, figuring he'd have a better chance wrestling me, but I managed to hit him with a hard uppercut, which lifted his head up enough for me to land two more into his forehead, which knocked him flat on his ass.

At that point everything else seemed to disappear except he and I. Blood flowed heavily from the back of his head where it hit the pavement, as I grabbed him by his shirt and his nuts, lifted him above my head and slammed him down hard on the top of his head. I felt someone tugging at my arm, but I snatched it away. As Bighead lay there, I speared my steel-toed Timberland boot-covered foot into the bone of his face over and over again as he began to convulse. My eyes were fixed on the bloody mess. Sweat poured from my bald head, down my face and spit formed in the corner of my mouth as Haleem and two young boys pulled me away from BigHead's body which was sprawled out on the pavement. "Come on man, you gonna kill that boy. Come on, get in your car man, before the police come." The word police definitely brought clarity to my thoughts, but I was still heated as hell. Haleem pretty much ushered me to my car, extended his hand, and with a warm smile he added: "As Salaam Alaikum Ahki" I got into my car and sped away back to the hotel.

I could barely see the road; my vision was still clouded with anger. I swerved in and out of the traffic until finally I pulled over to try and calm myself. I sat there behind the wheel for about an hour before I got out to walk it off. Halfway up the block I saw Victor, a guy I knew from Uptown. He recognized me immediately. "Heyyy Raheem, what up yo!" He said, wideeyed and smiling. "It's been a long time, brother. How you been?" I could see that Victor was cuffing a stem in one hand and a lighter in the other. "I'm good Vic, let me hit dat."

Victor and I ended up smoking crack and sniffing dope for five days straight. I ended up falling asleep behind the wheel of my car. I woke up with rabbit ears for pockets, and Victor was long gone. I didn't even look for him to get the few hundred dollars back that he obviously stole from me. I figure he would have either smoked and sniffed it up by the time I caught up with him, or he would tell me a lie so outrageous that I would end up doing something stupid to him and end up back in prison. "Fuck it" I thought. "Charge it to the game."

I had fucked up, again. And I knew that I had to do something. That fear kicked in. The fear of repeating that cycle of go to prison, come home, get high, commit crimes, and go back to prison. "The story of my fucken life," I thought. But this time I gotta do something different. I gotta at least try.

I had spent a very long time in some sort of jail or institution. In moments of clarity and sobriety, I had often dreamed of the opportunity to change my life. I had imagined what it would take to do that. To live and enjoy life like other people did. However, I struggled to find in my thoughts what it was. I knew money was an issue, but I knew for my life to flourish I needed something else, something more. Perhaps even something intangible. I had always known that I was broken, that something inside of me was lost or inept. I bought into the idea that a piece of my psyche did not believe that I could achieve happiness in its true form. I sometimes even thought that I was not made by the Creator to be happy in the "normal people" sense. I thought perhaps I was born to be the crackhead, criminal, dope fiend that I have always been. And the only place I may find a remnant of happiness was at the bottom, with the rest of the people who were like me. So, I had never tried to live. But this time, I was gonna at least try.

I went to the hotel, gathered all my things, the loot that I had left, and sat in my car calling rehabs. I wanted to put some distance between this last episode of me using, so that maybe I could get back on track. After a few calls I found a spot in Atlantic City.

CHAPTER 19

Stay Focused

I arrived at John Frost Rehabilitation Center facility at 9:00 a.m. As I pulled into the parking lot on Pennsylvania Avenue, two men exited the side door. One man appeared to be an employee of the facility; he wore a shirt and tie. The other appeared to be a resident; he wore jeans, sneakers, and a t-shirt. The pair greeted me as I exited the car extending their hands. "My name is Charles Dennis, and I am a primary counselor here. And this is Omar, our senior house Captain." He cordially announced. "How you doing. My name is Raheem Akmadir-Nahsif, and I..." "Great," Mr. Dennis interrupted. "We are happy to welcome you into our family. Omar will help you with your things, show you your room, and show you around. I'll meet up with you to talk with you later." Mr. Dennis said, as he shook my hand and entered, we the building.

I was amazed at how big the building was on the inside because looking at the building from the outside it didn't it didn't appear nearly as big. There was an auditorium, a gym, a library cafeteria and a sitting area for the clients to sit down and do homework and/or read. I was also surprised that there were so many women there. I didn't realize that it was a coed facility. Everybody seemed to interact and be cordial with each other. I later found out that most of the residents there were in relationships. But at the time, that didn't really matter to me because I was laser focused at this point and all I wanted to do was get myself together, get my mind right and try to create a life worth living.

I met with my counselor the following morning, Miss Agnes. She was an older white lady who had just moved into town from Utah. She was nice but she basically talked more about herself than me. I assumed she would want to explore what my core issues were. I mean I didn't know, but I expected that a counselor would be the one to talk with a resident to find out what their real issues were other than drugs. Granted, drugs would probably be the primary issue with anyone entering a rehab with an active addiction to drugs, however there had to be, at least in my case, an underlying issue that made me feel that drugs were the answer to my problem. I knew that drugs helped me to forget my reality, however I needed to find what was it that made me think that it
was OK to forget my reality rather than deal with it.

Needless to say, I thought Ms. Agnes was useless. Besides, I caught her looking at my crotch area way too many times. Each time I met with her it felt like I was being interviewed for a date rather than counseled for drug addiction.

Some of the residents there liked to attend NA meetings in the area. Some of the NA members often came to the facility to have what they called (H & I) Hospitals and Institutions meetings with us inside the facility. I appreciated the people who came in because they appeared to be authentic in their attempts to help us; and a lot of the stories they told about themselves were in a lot of ways identical to my own life. So, I appreciated it when they came in. They made me feel that I was not the only one in the world who had endured such tragedies and trauma in life. I felt maybe these people understood me and could perhaps help me find the solution to my problem.

I signed up for the 90-day stay and wasn't really interested in the long-term program that was offered. I had called Nola and explained the situation to her before I checked in. She sounded a bit irritated. However, she asked me to take better care of myself.

I felt like I had some money already put away and I knew that I could find a place to live with this money, so I felt like all I really wanted to do was get some distance between me and the drugs and then I would restart my life.

The residents there were pretty cool. Everyone pretty much did their own thing. A bunch of them were coupled up in relationships, always doing things together. I mostly kept to myself. I felt like if I focused on me, the likelihood of me getting my shit together was better, as opposed to me focusing on some woman and be distracted from what my goal was.

After about 30 days of being there some people came in from Legal Aid to educate us about our rights and benefits of being a low-income community. They all talked about how Legal Aid would help us with any legal issues that we may have.

One of the women giving the presentation was fantastically beautiful. She was at least ten years younger than me, I imagined. She was short, brownskinned, with phenomenally thick black hair. Her lips were full, and soft looking. I could not take my eyes off her.

"Sorry, I didn't get your name," I lied, as I walked up to her presentation table. She smiled a wide, beautiful smile, displaying a mouthful of beautiful white teeth. "Evelyn," she said. "My name is Evelyn." "It's a pleasure to meet you Evelyn," I said in my most sincere effort to imitate Barry White's voice, while taking hold of her soft hand and gently shaking it and looking into her warm, big, brown eyes. "My name is Raheem." "Nice to meet you Raheem," she cooed as she eased her hand out of mine.

I asked Evelyn a million questions about her, her life, her family, her dreams. I suspected she was trying not to be rude, so she answered a few. But I could feel that Evelyn was feeling me just as much as I was feeling her. While they were gathering their things to leave, I asked Evelyn if she could supply me with her business card, in case I had any questions. She smiled and slid one across the table and smiled coyly.

From that day on Evelyn and I talked on the phone and wrote letters to each other nearly every day. She talked about her aspirations, and I shamelessly talked about mine. She was 10 years younger than me, however I was amazed at her sense of maturity. I could talk to her about any and everything and I didn't feel judged or ashamed. I appreciated and looked forward to our conversation.

During one of those conversations when she came to visit me, she asked me why I didn't have any children. I honestly answered her with "I have always been in jail, or maybe I can't produce. I don't know. But I would love to have a baby with you," I chuckled nervously. She responded seriously, "The only way I'm gonna have another child (she had two children) is if I am married."

I looked her right in the face and said, "I'll marry you." She laughed, looking in my face deeper trying to gauge if I was serious. "I'm sseriou," I said softly. I got down on one knee, simultaneously taking off the silver initial ring I wore on my finger and slid it on to hers. "Will you marry me?" "Yes, I'll marry you," she said as she hugged me tight and began to cry on my chest.

A week later I was discharged from the program. A week after that we were standing in front of the Iman getting married. My Mom was ecstatic, and she adored Evelyn. So did my Dad and sisters. My entire family was happy that I had made the decision to get my shit together and begin to do what responsible grown people did.

I used some of the bread I had left to rent and furnish an apartment for us. I got myself two full-time jobs (Trump Plaza Casino and Sid's Furniture Store) to ensure the bills were always paid. Although I was not used to working, I was determined to build a life. But what I did not realize and continuously tended to forget is that the upkeep of personal responsibility is dependent upon the ability to manage how I feel.

Working two jobs had begun to take a toll on me. I was always tired and felt overworked. I fooled myself into thinking that I was not enjoying the fruits of my labor and that I should be celebrated for my hard work. Like I should be more than recognized for doing what grown responsible people do. "I'm 'bout to go reward myself," I boasted inwardly.

As a drug addict, I would always know where to find drugs. I could spot an active drug addict 50 paces in the dark. Although we differ in sickness and rate of recovery, we are all of the same kind.

I ventured into a part of Atlantic City called Back Maryland. This part of town was notorious for violence and drug use. I had heard about this area from my coworkers but never thought that I would end up being there. My co-workers always seem to have war stories about this particular area. The stories were always entertaining and sometimes fascinating.

One evening after work I asked my co-worker if she needed a ride home. I knew she would say yes, because she always caught the jitney. I dropped her off at her front door and watched her go in. I then drove around the corner to park the car. In the middle of the next block, I noticed a bunch of younger dudes playing loud music. Nearby, was a crowd of not-so-young people who appeared to be counting their money and fiddling around in their pockets as if they thought they had more than what they counted.

I got out of the car and made my way over toward that crowd. "Yo, who got it?" I questioned nonchalantly. "Got what?" a very skinny, ashy-faced man answered. "Who you?" he asked curiously. "You asking 'bout the wrong shit, Nigga," I shot back, grinning. I pulled out $80 from my pocket and said, "I'm trying to get a couple bags of diesel," I added. "I got you." "The young boy with the red hat got the monster," the ashy-faced man reported," adding, "He got the hard, too. C'mon."

I bought two bags of dope and five dimes of crack. And I bought the ashy-faced man one of each. I walked back to my car, stomach bubbling with anticipation all the way. I also thought about the ride I was about to embark on. One episode was never enough for me. I usually had to ride this drug-using train until the wheels fell off. I couldn't just use this one time and call it a night. I had to go all in, all the time. I pondered the fact that I would be sacrificing my jobs, the relationship I had with my wife, and my well-being. But that was a fleeting thought. I cracked open one of the bags of dope and snorted all of its contents with one swift motion. A warm euphoric feeling enveloped my body in seconds. I sat there for a long while…. Grooving.

My relationship with my wife began to suffer due to my use, the loss of both jobs, and my physical appearance had begun to decline. I had lost 10 pounds, and I mostly ran the streets all day, every day. Within a months' time I had regressed rapidly and begun to fail everyone miserably. Especially myself.

One evening I was preparing to head to Back Maryland when Evelyn sat beside me on the bed. She stared at me for a time (I saw her in my peripheral) before she handed me the at home pregnancy test. I looked at it to find the results were positive. Everything in my conscious mind was happy with this information. In fact, I'm sure I was ecstatic. But drugs had altered my emotions so badly that my body could not muster the feeling.

I wanted a child for a number of reasons. I knew I would be able to nurture a child and give it what I felt I did not get in my childhood, I would give it unconditional love, show it how to be responsible, and practice self-respect. I would teach it to be God- fearing and humble yet be firm in its convictions; to be resourceful and independent. I would even teach it how to protect themself physically if ever it came to that. I would show them how important education is, both academically and in the street.

I was so mentally psyched, yet the actual emotion of extreme happiness eluded me. The only emotion that was ever always easy for me to feel and express was anger.

I had dreamed about this day for years, and I fantasized that I would be so overwhelmed with emotion that I would cry. However, the best I could do was an embrace. I held Evelyn in my arms for a long while and kissed her face. I told her that I was so happy, and the Creator answered our prayers. She kissed me back and cried softly in my chest. I could hear her softly repeat "Alhamdulillah" (All praises be to God). I wanted to share in this cry with her, this blessed moment, this moment in my head that I understood intellectually and was ecstatic to have but could not feel. "What the fuck is wrong with me?" I yelled inwardly. "How are you so broken?"

My son Raheem was born on 6/30. He was the most handsome baby that I had ever seen. I scooped him up in my arms after the nurses had cleaned him up and I recited the Al-Fatiha prayer in his ear. I kissed his forehead, and I prayed for myself in that moment as well, asking the Creator to guide me. To fix me so that I could be everything this boy needs to become the man that he will need to be. I asked for this so humbly and desperately; from the depths of my soul, I begged. And then, I began to cry.

During the time that I had begun re-using drugs I had done such shameful and irreparable damage to my marriage. We both decided that it was best that we move on. However, I was determined to take care of my son, even if only from a distance. He was six months old.

I moved back to Passaic with my mother. Soon after I checked into another rehabilitation program "Focus Point," trusting that my heartfelt prayer in Atlantic City would somehow come to fruition.

I was not going to give up now. I felt that my son had given my life meaning. My life seemed to have purpose, and I did not want to fail. I needed to get this right this time. I did not want to be that Dad who was not a part of their child's life. However, I knew that to do that I'd have to become a better person. But.... How do I do that? All that I knew how to be was a conniving, manipulating, angry, otherwise emotionally numb dope fiend, crackhead, criminal.

This rehab was smaller but appeared to be more structured. The counselors seemed to be more invested in the clients. The counselors would take the time to sit down with a client and talk to them one-on-one when he/she appeared to be having an issue or behavioral problem, and they would often talk to the clients like normal people as opposed to an "addict".

I was assigned to a counselor named Steve Jackson. He disclosed immediately that he may or may not be a recovering addict. He was. He talked to me as if he knew me. He would tell me about the struggle I would face in life if I wanted to stay clean and increase the quality of my life. He reported that this would not be easy, but it would be well worth it.

Steve was also very funny, which kept the clients interested in what he was saying during his groups. He was funny, but in a relatable way. He would give a scenario which required the client to say what he or she would do in that situation. He would imitate (demeanor and mannerisms) the active drug addict in the most hilarious but realistic way.

However, he was also very serious and poignant when he talked about change. He said that if an addict wanted to change his/her life they would have to change everything about themselves.

I asked Steve during an individual session, "How do I change everything about myself? All I know how to be is who I am." He countered with questions of his own: "Raheem, do you think you are a good person? Do you think you do the right things for the right reasons, or do you think you are as greasy as a gas station mop?" We laughed hard about the gas station mop part of the question. He continued: "Raheem if you answered that question with the latter, then, you must start change with the little things. If you are used to walking past a crumbled piece of paper on the floor, pick it up. If you are not used to making your bed in the morning, make it up, and if you are not used to holding the door open for people, hold the damn door," he added humorously. All of these small things that you don't normally do will increase your sense of pride, self-worth and determination to do the right thing. Then, ultimately the change will show up in the more significant parts of your life. You will find yourself paying your bills...on time. You will find yourself saying 'No' when you would usually say 'Yes,' you will end up giving when you would usually be taking. All of which will increase the quality of your life. I guarantee this." All of what Steve said to me was intriguing and motivating. I wanted to try. I was desperate.

During the dinner meal I noticed a woman floating into the cafeteria area. I mean, she was walking but the way she walked, she appeared to be floating. She seemed to have this glow about her, her aura seemed to be intoxicating, intriguing, alluring. I asked the two people sitting next to me who this woman was. One said, "She's an aide. She only works on the weekend. She comes in and gets the people who the doctor needs to see." The other said, "She also conducts HIV testing. Her name is Florida."

I couldn't wait until my time for this woman to come and get me. She was phenomenally attractive. Not only because of her very big, beautiful behind and her brilliant smile. But also, in the way that she talked to people. She spoke to the clients respectfully and sincerely; her voice was melodic. She appeared to speak to people as if she genuinely cared about who the person was, where they came from, and their wellbeing. Her voice was soothing; it had an air of hood, yet she spoke very professionally; which made the clients feel comfortable talking to her.

I had just finished doing 10 sets of pull-ups in the bathroom and was headed back to my room to get my shower stuff to take a shower. "Excuse me young man," this sexy voice caressed my ears, "can I speak with you for a second?" I already knew who it was. I flexed my chest muscle before turning around. "Hey Ms. Flo. Sure, how can I help you?" I responded in my sexiest basstone voice. She appeared to be looking slightly away from me, avoiding eye contact. "I got a few questions for you, and we have to conduct a quick test. Can you follow me?" she asked, almost over the top professionally. "Anywhere in the world," I said under my breath, as I followed her into the examination room.

The fragrance that filled this room was more than intoxicating. I had not ever smelled anything like this on a woman. This fragrance evoked a certain energy inside me. I was overwhelmed with this energy that seemed to stir from somewhere deep inside me. It was not lust, well, not only lust, but it was more of a yearning, thirsty, drawn-to energy that I had never experienced.

"Damn!!" I said, not able to control myself. "What is that smell you're wearing?" I asked excitedly. "Excuse me?!" she responded, trying not to blush and trying hard to maintain the professionalism. "No offense Ms. Flo. But that fragrance you're wearing is absolutely astonishing!! I've never smelled anything like that before. And, it seems to have this weird effect on me," I confessed. "What?! She responded with a hint of concern. "No," I said, chuckling, trying to assure her that I wasn't a pervert. "What I mean is; it seems to have like a pheromone effect." Again, trying to hide the blush and smile by avoiding eye contact. She proceeded with the medical questions.

I resisted the urge to ask her a million personal questions. However, when she completed swabbing the inside of my mouth for the HIV test, I asked the name of the fragrance she was wearing and if I could get a closer whiff. She didn't answer, she continued to shuffle the papers she was handling. I leaned toward her and positioned my nose as close as she would allow and took a deep inhale. "Oh, my goodness!!" I exhaled. Whatever it is you're wearing Ms. Flo should be illegal, 'cause this may make people fall in love against their will," I smiled. "Thank you for your time, Mr. Raheem," she smiled as she nodded toward the door for me to exit the room.

I thought about Ms. Flo all night. She affected me like no other woman ever had. Her style, her grace, her authenticity was beyond my comprehension. She seemed stress free and unbothered every time I saw her. And that walk she walked, it was floating, she floated when she walked. I couldn't wait to see her the following week.

I had this indescribable attraction to Ms. Flo. Almost like a stalker, I thought. I mean, not only was I physically attracted to her, but I was stimulated by her calm, warm, and tranquil demeanor. And the way she talked, the content of her conversation was always filled with an interesting wealth of knowledge and information expressed in a way that suggested that she had firsthand knowledge of the darkness and horror of the world that I was used to, yet the joy and peace of mind of not ever having experienced a bad day in her life. It was baffling, but absolutely intriguing.

Flo called me to the office to read the HIV test results. She informed me the results were negative and asked if I had any questions. I told her that I did not have any questions about the test, however, I had a question I wanted to ask her. She looked up from the papers she was reading, with a nonchalant expression, "Go ahead." A bit stunned by her reply (she had always been so guarded), I stammered "Are you married?" "Why do you ask?" she said flatly. Stammering again, "Just curious." "Maybe you should not be concerned about that Raheem. Maybe you could take a look at how you will stay clean. I can tell you Raheem that the way to get and stay clean is to get gut-level honest with yourself about why you use, what makes you want to continue to use, and what will it take for you to become tired of using. I'm not trying to be mean Raheem. I am only trying to give you some information that may help you save your life."

"I've heard you say that you have been using for a long time. Well, you may need to address the reasons why. You may need to get with some people that will help you find you. Some people just like you who can identify with the same issues that you have. Some people who have surrendered to the past, gained some acceptance with what they cannot control, and acquired some hope for the future. I ain't gonna tell you staying clean will be easy... it may be very hard. But what I can tell you is that it will be worth it. However, it is a matter of how bad you want it. How bad do you want to live differently, and what are you willing to do to maintain a new way to live."

I stood there with my mouth open. I was amazed that this was the first time I had ever heard her say so much. And it was clear that she was indirectly revealing that she was a recovering addict. Also, she was speaking to me like she was personally invested in me. In that moment I did not know what to think or how to feel. I know Ms. Flo intended to give me useful information, But I wondered if she knew that she had just turned me on to the fucken 10th power. I was appreciative of the life-saving information that she provided, but I was turned on because I did NOT detect a sexual attraction to me coming from her.

Usually when a woman expressed any kind a concern for me, I could always spot the sexual attraction immediately. Flo's apparent disinterest in me ironically turned me on, because I imagined that even if she was good at masking her attraction for me, her genuine interest in my quality of life appeared more important to her. That for me, was mind blowing.

Focus Point had proven to be advantageous to me because it allowed me to examine myself at "gut-level," enabling me to see what my limitations were. Mostly, I deduced that my insecurities came from the trauma I had endured from Broom Hilda.

I believed, at least on some level, that I was not as smart as I wanted to be. I believed the only asset I had was my sexual prowess, and that I was inherently a bad person. I mean, consciously, I did not totally buy into that thought, but subconsciously it ate away at me, as demonstrated by my actions.

I had been at Focus Pointe for 31 days and was looking forward to leaving and getting on with building a life for myself. I had developed a respectful relationship with Ms. Flo, and the animalistic attraction to her had matured into a sincere appreciation and interest in all of who she was. I wanted to know her completely.

My discharge from Focus Point was on a Saturday. I was happy to see Flo before leaving. I slipped into the office she occupied when she worked and asked if I could get one more whiff of that pheromone fragrance she wore. She laughed light-heartedly but did not object to me leaning closer to her to inhale her neck. "Damn!" I exhaled with a pleasure-filled smile on my face. In almost a whisper I said, "I'd like to see you outside of here." The blushing smile instantly disappeared. Pensively, she replied, "Well, the only way you'd probably ever see me would be at an NA (Narcotics Anonymous) meeting. My home group is on Tuesday nights at the Veteran's Hospital in Newark." I smiled so big and wide I thought my face would crack.

I was excited about the possibility of embracing her and telling her how grateful and honored I was to know her. And even more elated about the opportunity to speak with her in a less restrictive way and tell her how much she turned me the fuck on.

I walked into the meeting about 10 minutes before it started. Flo was engaged in banter with the woman who sat at the table with two men whom I suspected led the meeting. Flo wore beige pants that enveloped all that behind perfectly. The brown sweater she wore equally held her voluptuous, caramel-colored body. Her shoulder length, braided hair bounced as she made her way to her chair.

I quietly made my way to the empty chair beside her. I leaned over, putting my mouth real close to her ear and whispered, "Damn, that fragrance you're wearing is amazing!" The look on her face was priceless. "Raheem!! Hi, I'm so glad to see you," she smiled, trying to conceal a hint of nervous excitement. "How are you?" she whispered, trying not to disturb the meeting. "I'm fantastic!" I beamed. "I didn't think you would ever show up," Flo admitted. "Oh, ye of little faith," I laughed. "We'll talk after the meeting." She blushed.

After the meeting Flo introduced me to a few people. She suggested that I get a few phone numbers from them to call in case of needing to run my thoughts or ideas past someone. As I walked around introducing myself and collecting numbers, she said her goodbyes. We exited the hospital together and walked slowly to her car talking and laughing.

Once we reached her car she asked if I had a way to get home. I told her that I was driving. She smiled. I asked if it would be okay if we talked a little while longer. She obliged. I opened the driver's side of her car for her and hurried around into the passenger side of her car.

We talked and laughed about everything under the sun. We talked about past relationships, love, fears, hopes, dreams, friendships, aspirations, staying clean, and life. We even laughed about some of our experiences with the horrors of active addiction. I felt so comfortable talking to Flo about myself. I did not feel judged no matter what crazy thing I told her about. In fact, most of the things I shared with Flo she would (on some level) say "Me too."

I also asked her about this glow she seemed to have about herself, this sense of tranquility she exuded. She attributed it to step work (working the 12 steps in NA). She said that I could have this glow as well. She suggested that I get a Sponsor, work the 12 steps of the NA program and find a God of my own understanding. I told her that I would.

But honestly, I would have told her that I would become a Chinese Missionary and travel to Africa to give out chickens to the Bushmen if it would have gotten me one more minute in her presence.

We exchanged numbers and made plans to meet for lunch at IHOP this upcoming Saturday. She gave me a hug, I kissed her on the cheek, and we departed. However, I was as excited as a kid in a candy store at the very thought of seeing her again.

We met at the Lyons Avenue IHOP. Flo was sitting at a table by the window when I arrived. I was amazed at how her aura/glow seemed to illuminate the entire place. She was gazing out the window smiling to herself, I noticed as I got closer.

"What are you smiling at?" I asked in my smoothest Billy Dee Williams voice. Flo looked up at me with a new, more energetic smile, "I'm just remembering the last times my sisters and I ate here. We used to eat here all the time. Still do, just not as much. They are funny as heck. Especially my sister Shirley-Ann," she chuckled. "Nice!" I replied. But I was hoping you were thinking about me."

As I sat across from her, she looked away bashfully and softly admitted," I was for a minute. I was thinking what it is about you that makes me go against my rule of never getting involved with a client…" "Well, we are not involved yet," I interrupted. "However, I absolutely hope to be. I find you extremely sexy, interesting, beautiful, sincere, and calming. And, I have never found so many of these qualities in a woman at the same time. Shit, it would probably take about three or four women to equal all the goodness you working with." I smiled.

"Thank you for saying that," she smiled, "but this is crazy!" "I have not been this attracted to any man since my son's father. In fact, I have not been in a relationship in years. This is crazy!" She smiled, this time a bit nervously.

"Look at me, Flo. It should be evident that I am extremely attracted to you. Not only physically, but I am attracted to every bit of who you are. The very thought of you makes my heart beat a thousand miles a minute. And the sight of you takes my fucken breath away. I think you are an amazing woman, and I would love to be a special part of your life," I confessed as I gently took hold of her hand. She smiled that nervous smile.

We talked for what seemed like hours at the IHOP. Then, she invited me to ride in her car (we left mine in the parking lot) as she gave me a tou of her city of Newark. We rode around for quite some time. Flo pointed out where she grew up, the location of the meetings she attended, and the street she lived on before we found a nice, secluded place to park in Weequahic Park.

There, we talked and laughed a bit more, until finally, I kissed her. "Amazing" is too weak of a word to describe the level of intimacy and passion that fueled that kiss. It felt like my entire being was being filled by her spirit. "Damn!!" I thought. "This shit right here better than any dope I've ever had."

Flo and I saw each other nearly every day after that night. I told her about all of my hopes and dreams as well as all of my fears. I didn't feel judged about my shortcomings, faults or past. She motivated me, made me feel like I could achieve anything. And when I expressed my issues with love (on every level) her response was simply, "Raheem, let me love you until you learn to love yourself."

That shit absolutely blew me away. I had never heard such a profound and sincere statement. I felt like I was home. And there was no other place in the world I would have rather been than with Flo.

I rented a place in Passaic. It was a studio on Dayton Avenue. It had a large room that I decorated as a living room/bedroom, a spacious kitchen that doubled as an office, and a small bathroom. The rent and security that I paid was all of any remaining loot that I had. But I was elated to have a place of my own for the first time, to bring my son to visit me on the weekends, and to be able to invite Flo.

I had discussed with Flo my dream of starting a business. Initially, I didn't know exactly what kind of business. I knew that I was a bit handy in terms of putting things together. And I knew people typically didn't like or got annoyed when they had to put things together for themselves. I figured most people would probably be willing to pay for that service if they could. "A handyman business!!" I thought. I ran the idea past Flo. She was excited for me. And when I located a used truck, she loaned me the $600 to purchase it.

For the first time in my life, I felt free, alive, and independent. I wanted to get cards and flyers made up advertising that I do it all: cleaning, painting, moving and assembling. I was a guy Friday, I thought. "That's it!!" I smiled to myself. That will be the name of my business, "Guy Friday." My catch phrase would be: "Somebody's Gotta Do It!" I laughed. I couldn't wait to get this printed on the side of my truck.

Flo had always supported and encouraged me to pick up my son every week. "A boy needs a man in his life to teach him how to be a man," she would say. So, I would be sure to get him each weekend. And he was always so happy to see me. I took him everywhere with me. Even to NA meetings. Everyone loved him. However, when there were jobs I needed to do on the weekend and could not take him with me, I sought the help of a young lady, Shirley, who lived in the building next to my Mom.

Shirley was young, maybe 25, married with five children: four boys and one girl. She was experiencing a difficult time with her husband. They had recently separated, and he wasn't really holding up his end as for as providing dough to help her with the children. So, I often offered to pay her to babysit for me. She never hesitated to say yes.

My son loved her and her children, especially her daughter Renea; they were the same age. Those two were inseparable. Whenever I attempted to take him somewhere he would always ask for Mama (Renea's nickname) to come. Mama was beautiful and always so full of laughter and energy. Every time she saw Raheem and I, she would run to us to give us a big hug. She was with us so much that people often asked me if she was my daughter. My heart would fill with love and appreciation that we were so blessed to have her in our lives that I would proudly announce, "Yes, that's my daughter." And, after a while, she would refer to me as her Dad. I loved it and treated her as such. In fact, she had me wrapped around her little fingers. Whatever she asked me for, or whatever I saw that I thought she would like, I got it for her. She was truly a "Daddy's girl."

Shirley's four boys were a little standoffish with me initially, which I understood. They were a little older than Mama and probably had fond thoughts and memories of their Dad. They weren't as receptive to me, at first. But they loved my son Raheem, and because they spent so much time with him, they would often see me, which probably made me not so bad. I loved them, and they began to love me, too. They were my boys, my sons, and I became their Dad.

Shirley and I ultimately established a mutual, respectable, understanding, and loving relationship. Quite frankly, I was a little afraid of her, at first. She was young (15 years my junior), sexy as a muthafucka, and spoke her mind without filter. I believed that if things were to become sexual with us it would probably alter the sound relationship I had with the children. I was wrong. I began to care about her, too. We looked out for each other, and she became one of my dearest and closest friends.

Flo was aware of the relationship I had with the babysitter's children. She understood that my son and I had begun to love those children. I regularly called them "my kids" in front of Flo. She never took issue with that. However, she suspected there was something going on with Shirley and me. She occasionally asked me if I was fucking her. I always said "No," but I imagined she knew I was.

CHAPTER 20

My biggest cheerleader

What's up Lady?" I said, as I kissed my Mom's face. "Hey Boy, where you been? I ain't heard from you in a few days," she questioned. "I've been all right, fixing up my place," I responded. "You got a phone, don't you?" she asked. "Yeah Ma, but I've been running around like a chicken with my head cut off putting together this business," I explained. "Hhm" she scoffed.

"I don't smell no food cooking in this joint, it's Sunday ain't it?" I said playfully. "I ain't doing no cooking today, shit, I'm tired," she complained. "Well, what you gonna to eat, Ma?" I asked, concerned. "I know how to throw something in the microwave if I get hungry, ain't nobody here but me," she reasoned.

I knew my Mom was feeling a little lonely. My sisters had moved out when they began having babies. Actually, I think my Mom was hoping I would come home from prison and live with her, not only because she worried about me and wanted me to have a place to stay, but because she was tired of living alone. However, she was ecstatic when I got married.

She was a member of the church now and went to bingo nearly every day, but I think she was still a little lonely. The last time she had a boyfriend that I knew of was about two years ago. But he drank, regularly, and since my Mom had stopped drinking years ago, they didn't have much in common, so they split up.

My father and his wife had broken up, too, about 10 years prior; so, my father began putting his Mack down immediately, all over town. He was still a handsome man at 60 something. He'd occasionally get back in my mother's door for a night or two, but she wasn't having him back permanently. She claimed he was too jealous and possessive. He also drank regularly.

"So, you ain't going to put nothing together for me girl?" I said playfully. "Hell no," she said seriously. I laughed. "Okay then, I'm going to a restaurant, you want to hang out?" "Do I want to hang out?" she asked, a little surprised. "Yeah, I'm going to Sylvia's in New York to get some down-home cooking, Girl, they make salmon, greens, potato salad, almost as good as yours," I lied. My Mom's was the best. She laughed, "Well, when you going?" "As soon as you get dressed, if you want to go. As a matter of fact, Ma, there's a play in New York on Broadway with Teddy Pendergrass and Stephanie Mills in it; let's go see that before we eat." "Boy, I ain't got nothing to wear to no damn play," she said, sounding as if she was trying to think of what to wear. "Well, Ma, we ain't going to visit the president," I chuckled. "You see I got on jeans, jacket, and boots, so just put on something comfortable." "Boy, I got to do something with my hair, and…." "Go ahead Ma, while you're getting ready, I'll call and find out what time the show starts." I interrupted. "Shit, all right," she surrendered, smiling and walked into the bathroom.

The play was called "*Your Arms Too Short To Box With God*" and it was playing at the Beacon Theater. The next show was at 6:00. We had plenty of time. "Boy, this is a nice damn car, I hope you ain't acting stupid out here messing around with people shit," my mother said, as she adjusted her seatbelt. "No, I'm not, I told you before, I bought this with the money I won," I said, like a little kid. "I sure hope you ain't lying. I hate to see you go back to that damn prison. I can't..." "I ain't going back their Ma, I ain't messing with nobody's stuff," I interrupted. "And why you carrying them knives I seen you put in your purse?" "To protect myself, you know these young boys out here are half crazy." We laughed.

The show was alright, I thought, but my mother loved it. She couldn't stop talking about it." Teddy Pendergrass know he can sing," she said as the waitress at Sylvia's brought our food. "It smells good," she said, like it wasn't supposed to. I laughed. My Mom ordered the fish and baked potato with salad. I had the barbecued beef ribs, mac and cheese, and salad.

"You see Cynthia since you been back? "Mom asked, causing me to choke on my grapefruit juice. "No," I said, "I ain't seen that hooker, and I don't want to. She better hope I don't cut her tongue out if I do see her. "You better leave that woman alone boy, before she have your ass back in that prison." "Nah, I ain't going to mess with her."

As my Mom ate, I kind of smiled and watched her, thinking how much I loved and admired her. Such a strong woman. All the things she had gone through in life, yet she still managed to keep her head up, with dignity, and overcome all of it. She was truly an extraordinary woman. Raising four children alone was rough enough, especially back in the day; being poor and an alcoholic, not to mention all the trouble and heartache I had caused her. I'd been insane by now if I'd had to endure that. I knew I couldn't take away all the pain I'd caused her, but I was definitely going to try to make up for it. I wanted her to live comfortably in her older years now without having to worry about anything. I intended on doing well with my business to make sure of that. "What you grinning about looking at me for?" Ma asked curiously. "Nothing," I smiled.

I loved my mother immensely. In fact, there was no other woman in the world that I could imagine feeling so strongly about. I knew that there was nothing in the world that I would not do for her. I cared about what she thought of me. I wanted to make her proud of me and to give her mind ease whenever she thought about me. I know a part of me wanting to make her proud came from the sense of guilt I felt for all the years I'd caused her grief by committing crimes, going to jail, and using drugs. I regretted the pain and shame I had caused her and wanted desperately to make amends by doing better.

"I love you Momma," I said lovingly in her ear as I firmly embraced her. My heart raced and my mind swelled with anticipation of her saying the same. "Okay, Boy, you take care of yourself out there," she responded with love in her voice. But I so desperately needed to hear the words from her mouth. I knew she loved me unconditionally. She had proven that many times. But for me, her speaking the words may have been life altering for me. Because I would have known long ago that love, real love is nurturing, pure, protecting, reassuring, inspiring, unlimited, and unrelenting. Everything my Momma was to me.

After I left my Mom's apartment, I went home, put the Best of Phyllis Hyman CD on, sat in my recliner and fell blissfully asleep.

CHAPTER 21

A new way to live

I went to the County Clerk's Office and obtained a DBA (doing business as) "Guy Friday," opened up a business account at my bank; and bought some of the necessary equipment that I may need to start my business. I'd rent stuff like the buffer or the vacuum cleaners, generators, dumpsters, etc. until I was able to purchase them. I bought mops, brooms, rakes, shovels, screwdrivers, wrenches, garbage cans, buckets, clothes, gloves, disinfectant, wood polishes, window cleaners: the whole nine. I wanted to be totally prepared. I did my own little research by calling other businesses to see what they charged for the basic cleaning, painting, or assembling so I'd know how to set my prices a few dollars lower.

Word of mouth is the best form of advertising. I was out early passing out flyers at every Lowes, Home Depot, Ikea, and supermarket I could think of. I'd start out at 8:00 a.m. on most days, working till 8:00 p.m. Everything was going well. I began making money hand over fist. I had employed my nephews, cousins, and one of my childhood friends, Stro, who was a Jack of all trades. This dude knew how to do everything from painting a room to building a fucken whole front porch. And he was meticulous.

We were making a lot of bread. And Stro was teaching me nearly everything he knew. I had already begun having feelings of accomplishment, like I was doing something worthwhile, honest and productive. I was extremely proud of myself.

Some nights, when I got home, the first thing I'd do was to call Flo because I had been thinking about her all day. I had been working so hard and meeting so many people that I did not find the time to reach out. But visions of her voluptuous, firm body interrupted my thoughts continuously. She came over to my place and we explored every inch of each other's body. Repeatedly.

She was my comfort zone, peace of mind, and safe place.

The humid, hot August air was thick. Some of my nieces and nephews felt like hanging out with me today, so, we headed out to Eastside Park in Paterson. I laid out the blanket I kept in my trunk in a nice shady spot under a tree, turned up the stereo in my car, and relaxed. As my family laughed and talked among each other I began thinking of the progress I'd made since I'd been back in Passaic, and I smiled. I enjoyed the day with my family and looked forward to many more of these days.

Guy Friday was doing extremely well, and I probably could have afforded a cheap storefront, which I imagined would be $1000 a month. But I didn't want to chance being strapped for cash too soon. I was frightened about the cost of insurance, overhead, utilities, and the fact that the location of a venue that I could possibly afford wouldn't be all that great.

Although I had only been in business five months, I already had a thriving business with a good reputation; a very nice place to stay; a nice car; and a nice piece of dough in the bank; I still wanted that venue: now! I was impatient. I wanted what I wanted when I wanted it. In prison, I had no other choice but to be patient. But now that I was in the world, doing what I always wanted to do, and the ensuing excitement was overwhelming.

Patience became a thing of the past. I felt like I needed to make up for all of the time I wasted doing drugs and going to jail. "Maybe I should start an additional business," I thought. One that I could tend to while I wasn't doing the Guy Friday thing. Easy, convenient and with little risk of losing money.

Haughtiness, immaturity, and greed began to invade my thinking. I began to think 40 was getting old, and I knew that all the years I spent in prison put a definite damper on the way my life should be going. I figured, at 40, I should have been well established in my line of business; keeping up payments on a house; with a wife and at least two kids. But the women I had met so far, not that I had been looking, were not able to provide or suffice for me. I reasoned.

Although Florida was amazing and had awakened parts of my emotional being that I had never known existed, I felt she was not interested in having any more children. Her son was grown. And she was about ten years older than me and probably not able to have any more children, I thought. Even in the midst of this thought, I knew it was irrational.

"Excuse me bro, what happening?" the young brother said, interrupting my thoughts as he stood there with an armful of clothes. "It's all good, man what's up?" I answered curiously. Yo, man, are you interested in some gear? I got Hilfiger, Donna Karan, Nike shirts and sets, check it out," he said, as he began laying some things out on my trunk. I glanced over a few things before I came across a nice pair of green Nike shorts like the pair I wore. "How much you want for these?" "Give me $10 for them. As a matter of fact, bro, I'll give you the shirt to go with that for $10, too? All right?" "Hold up, what else you got?" I questioned, excited that I was getting a deal. "I got a lot of shit, check out this Hilfiger shirt. I'll give it to you for $15. And since you going to get the Nike shorts and shirt, I'll give you everything for $30," he boasted. "All right," I accepted. "Yo, I got three kinds of shirts too, you want to check these out?" he presented. "No, no, I'm all right, this is all I want right here," I said, as I separated $30 from my wad. "Good looking out G, peace," the young brother said, and departed.

I looked at the things over again before putting them in my trunk, then sat down and went back to cooling out with my family. When suddenly, it hit me: I could do that. I could sell clothes! The clothes these brothers and sisters were selling were called "knockoff" imitations. Nike, Hilfiger, Dickies, etc. People usually bought these clothes from New York at nearly-nothing prices; then brought them back to New Jersey and sold them at double, sometimes triple, the price. Everybody's doing it, I could too. But then I thought, "If everybody's doing it, why would I want to do it?" The first lesson I had learned from Steven C. Harper's book, *Starting Your Own Business:* "Never enter a market that is already crowded with competition." Damn! I thought. On damn near every corner of every town near me there were at least two or three people selling clothes; sometimes they even had the same shit. I'd just be another.... "Hold up," I thought, "I could take this shit to another level. I don't have to stand out on the block, or in a park; and I ain't got to sell the same kind of things everybody else is selling."

Number two lesson listed in the book said the reason most businesses fail is because the business didn't offer exactly what the people wanted. Shit, I could buy top notch clothes and sell them to people who own clothing stores. Before I went to prison, I used to steal the most expensive suits, dresses, purses, and shoes and sell them to drug dealers and store owners. I could sell them to people who I knew wore those kinds of things, and who had the loot to pay for them.

I often sold the things I had stolen at office buildings, to women at beauty salons, outside doctor's offices, restaurants, the whole nine. Besides, they always wanted something for basically nothing. "Hold up," I thought, grinning, knowing I had a good idea, and began to fold up my blanket. I got to go home and map this shit out. I gathered my nieces and nephews, dropped them off, and went home.

First thing Monday morning, I drove down to the County Clerk's Office and got a second DBA; then to City Hall to get a Peddler's License; and finally, to the bank, to open up an additional account under my new business name: Exclusive Clothing. I was so eager to get my new business started, the next week, whenever I got a spare minute in between jobs, I'd either be getting business cards or flyers made up for Exclusive Clothing, or I'd be in New York asking questions and lining up connections to purchase products.

I met a guy named Jose who took me to a building on Orchard Street, which was a 17-story, factory-type building where the owner sold everything from tube socks to silk shirts and dresses, at unbelievable prices. On the first few floors of the building were hundreds of Asian, Hispanic, and other immigrants working; either making, pressing, tagging, boxing, and/or shipping the clothes. The other floors, as far as I could tell, we're used to display and store the clothes. I was basically amazed at this operation. My first thought was whoever owns this spot has got to be a rich motherfucka.

Jose explained the operators would make up pant suits, shirts, dresses, etc., which came very close to how the popular designers designed: like Versace, Gucci, and Dior. Then, the purchaser of these imitations could buy whatever designer labels he wanted and have them sewn on himself, somewhere else of course, because the fact that whoever owned the spot didn't put any imitation labels on the clothing that was being made there, made it a perfectly legal-to- do business.

I was completely amazed. Shit, I thought, all that time I was robbing people and wrestling them to the ground to steal their money. I could have been robbing them the American way. I laughed to myself.

Men's suits were $75 apiece, but you had to buy a minimum of six. Ladies' suits were $60, and dresses were $40, all at half a dozen minimum. I explained to Jose that I only needed a couple of each, as samples to see how well they sold. And if I sold fast, I guaranteed him I'd be back for at least a dozen of each. He obliged.

Nola and I had remained friends. She and I would talk on the phone occasionally. I believe she understood the age dynamic between us. Although we never spoke in depth about it, it was obvious that a committed relationship between us would never work. However, she always wished me well. In fact, the day after I purchased the clothes from New York, Nola suggested that I call her brother to see if he wanted to buy anything.

The next day I sold the two "Ralph Lauren" suits to Nola's brother, a local businessman, at $200 apiece. Two days after that, I sold the women's suits and dresses to a woman at a beauty parlor in Nutley for $480. I was ecstatic to have sold the clothes so fast, with very little effort. I was even more excited by the subtle implications that I had stolen the clothes. "Yeah man, these are some good suits here brother," Nola's brother said. "If you ever get your hands on some more and need to get rid of them quick, just come on down and I'll take them off your hands."

"Oh my God, these are beautiful," the little white lady at the beauty parlor said. "When you're ever able to get away with something in beige or green in the same style, I'll be more than happy to purchase them, as long as the price remains the same," she added. I mean, I was aware of how excited people were by the idea they were getting a good deal, especially when they thought the person who was giving away the deal was desperate. Or how excited people got when they thought they were doing something slick: bending some sort of rule or getting something for nothing. I was aware how the success of my business could be based on that fact, but I also didn't like it.

After I purchased two dozen men's suits and two dozen women's suits, and several dresses from Jose's spot on Orchard Street, I persuaded and paid a young woman to make up a thousand labels which read "Exclusive Clothing." I had a label sewn in every garment I bought from them. I also found a small plastics shop on Delancey street. I had black garment covers made up bearing the name "Exclusive Clothing" in bold white letters. I even went so far as to have receipts made to give to anyone who wanted one.

I carried my Peddler's License, DBA, and business cards everywhere I went. But still, the fact that I sold my wares from the van I had purchased represented an air of "illegal," which drew people to me wherever I went. Which was cool with me, of course, as long as they were spending. I was convinced that I could sell a prostitute a day off on payday in Times Square.

My sales pitch was, for the most part, flawless. I'd always been phenomenal when it came to talking people into buying things from me during my drug days, and it seemed I hadn't lost it. On some occasions, when the folk that I approached would buy from me, I'd give them a shirt or a dress or something, along with a few of my cards, at no charge; providing they promised to wear the garments to work, and let a few of their co-workers and friends know where they got them. This would ultimately cause the person whom I gave the garment to call me within a couple of weeks with an order to purchase something.

Fact is, the sales pitch I used during my drug days was fueled by my desperation for money to get drugs, as opposed to now where my sales pitch was fueled by my thirst for success. The fact of knowing that I've done something for myself, by myself.

Draped in an almond-colored Hugo Boss, "authentic suit," and brown, baby croc shoes; green and brown paisley silk tie; a crisp white shirt; and gold-framed Hugo Boss glasses, I waited for the elevator in the ADP building in Nutley. Actually, I wasn't really waiting for the elevator. I had noticed a tall, thin, well-dressed woman, who looked to be in her late twenties early thirties, enter the building and I was waiting for an opportunity to solicit her business.

"Hello, how are you this afternoon?" I asked the well-dressed woman, flashing her a big smile. "I'm fine, thank you, how are you?" she answered, enthusiastically. "Great, great. I'm Raheem," I said extending my hand. "Nice to meet you, I'm Laura." "It's a pleasure to meet you, Laura." "Thank you," she said. "Do you work here at ADP?" she asked, smiling. "No, actually, I'm just here to see a friend about a few things. Laura, I hope I don't offend you, but you have the most beautiful hair," I interrupted whatever she was about to say. "Why thank you!" she exclaimed surprised and turning as red as a stop light. "It looks so full and healthy; you must get it done professionally and regularly." "No, she said, clearly flattered. "I do it myself." "Is that right?!" trying to sound surprised. "It's absolutely beautiful. Kind of gives your face a radiant glow." "Thank you," she chuckled. "Ah," I said, trying to sound embarrassed, "I know I might be crossing the line a bit here Laura, but do you mind if I touch it?" "What?!" she said, beaming with excitement and embarrassment, as she chuckled and looked around. "I'm sorry, Laura, I didn't mean to embarrass..." "No, it's okay, go ahead, you can touch it. Sure, go ahead." I took a handful of her hair in my hand and kind of let it fall in between my fingers. "Oh, that's nice and soft." "Thank you!" "It feels like blonde silk." "Thank you," she chuckled, looking away embarrassed.

But as soon as she looked up again, I put my game down. "Laura, I'd like to show you something," I said, as if I just stumbled upon the most brilliant idea in the world. "Can you just stay right here a second? It won't take me long; I just have to run out to my car a minute." "Oh, Okay," she said, kind of confused.

I fixed a very proud and excited smile on my face as I re-entered the building with three silk dresses across my arm. "I think this beautiful black silk dress would look absolutely lovely on you. You're a 5-6, right?" "Yes, she answered, even more confused. Not wanting to totally spook her, "I'm sorry, Laura, what am I thinking," I said, apologetically, as I gave her my card. "I represent Exclusive Clothing, and after getting an eyeful and a handful of your beautiful hair, I couldn't help imagining how completely gorgeous you'd look in one of these dresses." She turned into a stoplight again. "Here, just let me sit this down and show you what I'm talking about," I said, as I walked over to the lounge area of the lobby. As I took the dress from its covering, her eyes lit up and she let out a gasp of approval as she fingered the fabric. "Lovely, isn't it?" I chuckled inwardly. "Yes, this is beautiful," she added. "Here, hold it up against you so I can see how it looks. She held it very close to her body up under her neck, then looked at me for my reaction which was: "Wow!" "Laura, that would look terrific on you," I said excitedly. "Let's see how you'd look in the brown one."

I gave Laura the same flattering remarks about each dress she held up against herself. I honestly thought she looked good in the olive dress. I'd never had the opportunity to have sex with white women, and the thought of her tall, thin body under mine did cross my mind quite a few times when she held the dresses up against herself. "I'll tell you what Laura, since I find you absolutely breathtaking, I'm going to give you the black dress at no charge, which costs about $300 in the finest stores throughout New York; provided you tell me when you think you'll be wearing it to work, so that perhaps I can cruise by and get at least one look at how many hearts you'll stop that day by simply looking fabulous." She chuckled. "And I'll let you have the other two at $180 apiece. Fair enough?" I proposed. "Okay," she agreed. "Let me see how much I have on me." She counted out $320. "I only have $320," she said, in disappointment. "That's okay, young lady, I'll put the other $40 in out of my own pocket," I smiled. "Thank you, Raheem. I can't wait to try them on." "I'm sure you'll be pleased." "Okay, so you have my cards?" "Yes, I have them," she said looking me directly in the eyes, with that Universal Woman Look, which said something more than buying dresses.

Normally, at that point I would be setting her up for the dick down. But I hadn't been with Flo in a few days, and I had her on my mind all day. There was no substitute for Flo. "All right then, if you or any of your co-workers or friends would like to purchase anything in the future, please feel free to call me. Exclusive carries virtually everything for men and women except shoes," I said. "Oh, okay!" she replied, as if she expected me to say something else. "It was a pleasure meeting you, Laura," I said, trying to sound sincere. "Same here. Bye-bye.

I stopped at the A&P Supermarket after leaving the ADP building to pick up some grapefruit juice and gum, before proceeding to Flo's house for some real lovin'. While paying for them at the checkout counter, in line in front of me was a young black brother paying for his goods. He held in his arms a little boy who was the spitting image of him. The little boy seemed to be smiling at me, then put his arms around his Daddy's neck and kissed his face. It reminded me of my son. I was missing him and wanted to see him badly.

When I got to Flo's house, she answered the door wearing an olive-green nighty. I embraced her and kissed her passionately. I whispered in her ear how much I missed her and how I was gonna make slow passionate love to her until she begged me to stop. She whispered back in my ear, "You better pack a lunch, cause I ain't never gonna say that!" We laughed, hard.

After what seemed like hours of hot, sweaty, passionate lovemaking, I began to tell Flo how much I missed my son and how badly I wanted to see him. I told her that I wanted to ultimately raise my son and help him become the man he would need to be in this world. I told her that I did not want to be a part-time Dad. I wanted to be present and active in his life. Flo adamantly suggested, "Go see your son."

I called Evelyn and told her that I would be coming to see Raheem on Friday. She suggested that I take him for the weekend to spend some quality time with him. I was elated at the idea of bringing him back to my place, cooking him breakfast, taking him to the park, and just talking to him.

After loading my son into the car seat, I drove down to Atlantic Avenue outlet area stores and bought him a bunch of clothes and toys. I was a beaming Dad all the way home. I stopped over Flo's house to introduce my son to her. He immediately liked Flo. They laughed and talked with each other for a long while.

Flo went into the fridge to find a snack for him. She returned with a bowl of large, juicy grapes. My son tore into those grapes like they were the best thing he had ever tasted. We laughed at how he seemed to shield the bowl with one hand (as to protect the grapes from us getting any) while he ate the grapes with the other hand. He was adorable. Flo fell in love with him too. I would often playfully inject myself into their conversation and play in order to get some airtime with either of them. They were inseparable.

When I took my son home, I would talk to him for hours, like he was grown and understood me. I would tell him about my plans to ultimately have him come live with me so that I could be in his life and teach him how to be a man. I would tell him how much I loved him and would sacrifice my life to protect and provide for him.

I remember one day telling him all of these things so poignantly that tears began to flow from my eyes. He wiped my tears, and with a concerned look on his face, he wrapped his tiny arms around my neck to console me. I couldn't help but laugh lightly, "Awwh, Daddy is fine, man. I'm okay. Daddy is just happy that you are here," I reassured him. He looked back at me with much less concern, smiled, and hugged my neck again. I began to pick up my son to bring him to my apartment nearly every weekend.

My professional life was blowing up. Things couldn't have been better. I had managed to rent a storefront on Lexington Avenue for a reasonably low price, a perfect location. It was clearly visible to traffic going and coming in all directions. I had three full-time, loyal employees who were capable of running things while I was busy with other work. I had work scheduled for months. People were stopping in regularly to patronize Guy Friday services.

Exclusive Clothing had only been in effect for six months, and in that time, I made several thousands of dollars. I had two young ladies who worked for me in two different Beauty Salons, selling the finest clothes, which brought in an average $1500 a week. Business was extremely good. It was so good that every so often I'd rent a double suite at the Embassy Suites hotel to show off my latest collections. Sort of like a fashion party/advertising show. The two young ladies who worked for me would wear some of the new dresses and suits around the party, changing periodically, while I wore one or two of the suits. The rest of the items would be displayed on mannequins, strategically placed about the Suites, or laid out across the beds.

I supplied shrimp and strawberry platters, Moet champagne, and soft jazz to put everyone in a festive mood. Not only was I killin' 'em with my clothes, I was also getting new info from the partygoers on how to possibly make more money with my businesses. Some of which was how to acquire foreclosed property in the area. In attendance were businesspeople of all sorts; more than willing to talk about their respective lines of work. I eagerly listened. Men loved to attend these parties, because they expected many women would attend. They were right. And women often invited me to their affairs; because I suspected, they wanted the opportunity to put their game down on me. This was fine with me, because despite their intentions, mine were to make money. And that I did. Diligently.

Initially, the fact that I was 39 years old and had gotten out of prison with nothing and no education to speak of was what motivated me to work hard to make my money and become successful. But now, because I had a child, and, I imagined, because I was no longer getting high, I worked harder; and in some way I got high by every successful business endeavor. From Monday to Saturday, I'd wake up at 5:00 a.m., workout, eat, shower, dress and then be out of the door by 7:00

to work with my cleaning/home Improvement, and clothing businesses till 8 or 9 p.m.

CHAPTER 22

I say yes, when I need to say no

Maxine was a tall, thin, very dark, Robin Givens-type young lady I had met at my latest showing at the Embassy. Her beautiful face and seductive, raspy voice I found very attractive. During the showings or any other business venture for that matter, I never mixed business with pleasure. However, I always gave the impression that I was interested completely in a prospective client, and I often give out my home number; but that was only to ensure a call.

I had evidently given my number to Maxine. "Hi, Raheem, how are you?" she cooed into the receiver, her raspy voice barely audible. "Fine Baby, who is this?" I replied curiously. "Maxine, you met me at your party at the Embassy the other night." "Oh, yeah, tall, dark, sexy sister?" I questioned. "That's me," she chuckled. "How can I help you Baby?" I asked, getting into business mode. "Well, you asked about the auctions held at City Hall." "Auctions?" "Yes, in regard to abandoned and foreclosed properties?" "Oh, oh, yes, I remember. I'm sorry Sweetheart, it's been a rough week," I apologized. "That's okay. Anyway, there's an auction on Thursday and there's a few properties you may be interested in."

"Is that right?" I said, concealing my excitement. "Yep, what are you doing tomorrow night? Maybe we can have dinner so that I can tell you what you'll need, and the things you'll have to do in order for you to qualify for assistance etc." "Well, what time is good for you?" I asked. "How's eight?" she asked. "Cool, where" I inquired. "Is Reuben's Supper Club, okay?" "Sure, I'll see you there," I said, impressed by her choice. "Okay," she said, and hung up.

I was very excited at the possibility of owning property. I'd heard a lot about how people bought property at these auctions for barely anything. Sometimes a two-family house as low as $10,000. The city would then help the purchaser renovate the property to meet its standards and laws; by extending loans and grants and whatever other kind of assistance is available.

However, for me, at that time, outside of not having the money to indulge in that type of venture, I was fearful that my criminal history would in some way hinder my chances to acquire one of these properties, or at least it may have shut down my chances for any kind of loan or grant. But now that I had more than enough loot to purchase property and the privilege of knowing someone who was involved in the intricate workings of this business process, I was more than confident that I was on the verge of yet another successful business venture.

I wasn't quite sure what kind of work Maxine did at City Hall, but the way she talked indicated she did something of importance. I didn't intend to fuck Maxine, thinking that it would prompt her to pull a few strings for me. I only intended to become cool with her and possibly establish a "one hand washes the other" business type of relationship with her. I mean, judging from what folks said about her and her attire the evening of my party, (she wore only top of the line clothing), I was definitely willing and able to add to her fine wardrobe, just as long as she was willing and able to assist me in owning something significant for the very first time in my life. Fair exchange wasn't a robbery.

Under different circumstances, I would have definitely pursued Maxine for my personal interest. I mean, she was fine as hell and had the roundest ass I'd seen in quite some time on a woman as slim as she was. Her deep chocolate skin and full perky lips gave her the look of someone I'd love to wake up to giving me head every morning. Only, her Robin Givens demeanor was the ultimate turnoff. She seemed a bit snooty and conceited, almost as if the people at the party, with the exception of my two employees and myself, were beneath her. She also gave off gold-digger vibes.

"Hello, Chocolate Woman," I smiled and sat down at the table to join Maxine. "You're looking delicious this evening," I complimented. "Why, thank you," she said in a tone that really said, "I know." "Have you ordered yet?" I asked, as I took in the ambiance of Reuben's. It was an absolutely beautiful place to eat. The large wall, built-in fish tank filled with tropical fish; and the plants, ceiling fans, cool breeze, and flowers which hung from the ceiling, gave the whole place a tranquil and calming effect. The plush carpet beneath my feet and the soft sounds of Coltrane gave me the comforting feeling of sitting in my own living room. "No, not yet, I waited for you, but I did order some wine," she said proudly. "I'm sorry, Maxine, I don't drink." "Oh?" she sounded disappointed. The waitress interrupted, "Excuse me, are you all ready to order dinner?" I ordered sea bass and spinach. It was good; but the salmon Maxine ordered must have been great, judging by the way she ate it, slowly and thoughtfully, putting each bite into her mouth like she was performing at a five-second peep show.

The conversation went surprisingly well. Maxine informed me that I need not worry about the auction or a loan if I did choose to purchase property, because purchasing property required that I had the money to pay for it, which I had. The fact that I owned two thriving businesses would virtually secure a loan, especially since the secured credit card that I had for the past year had established some aspect of credit for me.

She further said that if I needed any help in regard to a cosigner, she'd be more than happy to do it for me. I was definitely impressed with her. But certainly, I knew that this kind of offer came with some fucking or sucking. Probably both.

As Max and I walked to her car in the parking lot, I thanked her again for the info and her offer. She seemed sincerely pleased with being able to be of assistance. "Okay, Sweetheart, good night. I appreciate everything, and I'll give you a call Thursday to let you know how things turned out at the auction." I said, as I held open her car door for her.

To my surprise, Maxine closed the car door, stood there with her arms folded, looking at me a few seconds before she spoke. "Raheem, I'm a very forward person and usually I say whatever is on my mind, and tonight is no exception. However, tonight I wanted to be passive and just see where tonight led me. But it seems to be leading me home, where I don't want to be right now," she spoke, softly. "Raheem, do you think that I asked you to dinner only to give you that info? I could have given you that on the phone! Hello!" she said, facetiously. "I'm attracted to you!" We both laughed. "Don't read me wrong though Raheem," she continued, "I don't take this position with everyone. I'm attracted to you, and I figure we're both adults. And from one adult to another, I don't want to go home alone tonight. I want to go home with you." She moaned and moved closer to me. I was extremely flattered, and I admired her honesty. Although I found Maxine very sexy, visions of Flo's face flooded my mind. I really cared about Flo. And I was certain that she cared about me more. I couldn't rationalize risking the ideal relationship I had with Flo for some pussy I didn't particularly want. I mean, I really wanted the business, the pussy, not so much. I mean, no doubt I had fucked for way less than what Maxine was offering, and I had never been opposed to fucking for something. But my feelings for Flo wouldn't be compromised.

I leaned forward and kissed her softly on the cheek, then whispered, smiling, "Maybe next time." As I leaned back, away from her, she reached up and held my face between her soft hands and slowly sank her sugary tongue deep into my mouth, moaning softly, hungrily. "I can't wait till next time," she cooed as she slid my hands in between her legs to reveal a sopping wet box. "Shit!!" I exclaimed with restrained excitement. "I'll follow you home."

Maxine's home was large and extremely immaculate. Beautiful fresh flowers and plants were practically everywhere, which gave her house a great sweet smell. Oriental rugs accentuated her glass and brass coffee table, and bookshelf; and carpet flowed throughout the rest of the house, as the finest contemporary furniture rested atop of it. She also had quite a few very nice paintings, but strangely, most were of white people. Her bedroom was especially large. The hot pink walls were almost entirely covered by large mirrors, even on the ceiling, and the king bed was draped in a black satin sheet and comforters.

Max turned on the stereo and commented that I should get comfortable. She excused herself into the bathroom. When she reappeared, she was wearing only a very sheer pair of thong panties and an even more sheer lace bustier. I knew right then that I wouldn't have to work out the next day because I was about to do all my working out as soon as she took one step closer to me!

Words escaped me as she floated towards me wearing the face of a hungry mountain lion, but little did she know, I was as hungry as a greedy bear after a long hibernation. Actually, it had only been 14 days since I had some sex, but it felt like an eternity. I couldn't use my right hand because I had sprained my wrist lifting a file cabinet.

Wrapped in a warm embrace, I passionately kissed her mouth and neck. Her smooth, deep chocolate skin glistened in the dim light. I caressed her soft body, slowly. She lay on her back, legs spread apart, while she guided my strong, big hands to her hot tenderness. My thick, hot tongue entered her waiting mouth, while my long fingers entered her. She held onto my wrist and began grinding her hips slow and deep onto my fingers. Her tenderness emitted heat and copious amounts of sweet juices. Her wetness dripped down my hand as she rode my fingers more vigorously and sucked my tongue into her mouth.

I needed my right hand to put on the condom, but her hands were locked around my wrist. I figured I'd help her along in reaching the first orgasm, then I'd be able to free my hand to put the condom on. I intended to slowly move my fingers in and out of her to match her strokes; but as soon as I attempted to, she said in a tone that actually scared the hell out of me, "Leave it right there. I'll tell you when to move it!" "Damn!" I thought, but I didn't move it, I left it right there until she had reached her orgasm.

After putting the condom on, I decided to have her from the rear first. I kissed her belly and hips lightly; softly pushing her body at the same time, to indicate that I wanted her to turn over onto her stomach. "Not yet, I don't want it like that yet!" she growled in a loud, nasty, frightening tone which damn near caused me to jump clean off the bed. "Fuck me from the front first, then I want to ride you, and then you'll fuck me from the back. Okay, Baby?" she said in a sudden soft tone, in an attempt to take the sting out of everything else she had said.

Ordinarily, I would have cussed her snooty ass out; or anybody else's out, for talking to me in such a tone. And because she seemed to be only interested in her pleasure, I'd ordinarily put my drawers on and scram. But that night she caught me at a time when I was, as I said, as hungry as a bear; and I wasn't about to leave before I got at least one off, dammit. Besides, I assumed she wasn't intending to be nasty and demanding in a rude kind of way, she didn't even know me like that. I assumed, like many other people who had certain kinds of desires and/or ways of communicating their needs when they're having sex; some were less subtle than others. Giving orders was something I guess she enjoyed doing. So, I ignored it. But I must admit, it definitely was an unpleasant experience. All of that "wait a minute, move this way, don't move like that, didn't I say this way, slower, okay, faster," drove me fucking crazy. She even told me to stop completely while I was in mid-flow and insisted that I follow her every command to the letter.

That's when I completely ignored everything she said, threw her legs on my shoulders, and thrust myself into her so hard and fast that our sweaty bodies slapping together sounded like loud claps of thunder. That is, until her body began to convulse; tears flowed heavily from her eyes, and she sank her fingernails deep into my arms, drawing blood. She emitted a high-pitched scream, which caused my ears to ring; before collapsing, completely exhausted, from her first-ever multiple orgasm.

I lifted myself from her still-trembling, unconscious body, got dressed and headed towards the front door with my chest poked out, grinning like a Cheshire cat, thinking, "How you like me now?"

When Flo visited me at my apartment the following night, I could barely look her in the face. I felt terrible that I had allowed my greed to guide me like that. It wasn't so much the sex, because sex with Flo was amazing. It was more about giving Maxine such phenomenal sex that she would give me anything I needed as it related to the auction process. I probably still subconsciously felt that this was all I had to offer of value. The vicious words of Broom Hilda, "You better hope that big black, funky dick of yours stay workin'. 'Cause if it evvver stop workin' ain't nan Bitch in the world gone want yo ugly ass."

Subconsciously, I still believed that I was not enough. I still believed that my intelligence, business savvy, abilities to think logically and/or comprehend were not enough. I still believed that no one would like me for who I was and what I had to offer as a person. I still believed I had to initiate sex into every situation to be accepted and wanted.

Max telephoned me every day after that evening and although I was flattered, by her persistence, we had absolutely nothing in common, except the sex, of course. She was totally into impressing people with what she owned, the things she did, and the places she went.

She'd even go so far as to try to tell me how to dress, how to talk and even what to order for dinner when we dined. I mean, I went along with it for a while because can't nothing inflate a man's ego like rendering a woman unconscious, during animalistic sweaty sex, and I was knocking her ass out at least once a month.

I felt some loyalty to her for helping me through the process of obtaining the eight abandoned apartment buildings I had purchased at the auction. She also had shown me several loopholes in regard to getting loans; which enabled me not only to get money to fix up the abandoned buildings I'd purchased; but also, to establish an agreement with the bank to purchase a foreclosed two-family house for my Mom.

So, when she asked me to come over to my place, I occasionally allowed it. We chilled and had sex there a few times. However, I insisted that she always called me before she came over. Sometimes she would, sometimes she wouldn't. When I checked her about not calling first, she would say, jokingly, "Why would I have to call my man's house before I came by?" "I'm not your man Baby, I'm your friend," I responded seriously. "You my man,

Nigga, you just don't know it yet." I had been seeing her for several months now. Although Maxine appeared to be joking, I got the sense that she believed that she would one day become my woman, no matter how many times I told her it was not going to happen.

One evening Max invited me to have dinner at her parents' house. I didn't object to having dinner with her parents, actually, I kind of looked forward to it, figuring her parents would more than likely be the place where I'd meet the real Max. Because it had been my experience that parents have a way of making their child be who they really are, at least around them.

But I was surprised when, instead of having dinner with her parents, I found myself in the middle of a virtual family reunion, only it wasn't a family reunion. Max had invited her aunts, uncles, grandparents, sister, brother, oldest friends and all of their children to her parents' home to announce her impending marriage: to me!!!! Shocked the hell out of me!

This woman stood up at the dining room table, straight-faced, and proceeded to tell everyone how she'd found Mr. Right, and how I had asked her to be my wife. "Mom and Dad," she said, with tears rolled up in her eyes, "this man has made me so very happy, in every way a woman could ask, and he loves me just as much as I love him: we're getting married. I want you to meet your future son-in-law." I damn near swallowed the whole chicken breast I had been eating. The room erupted with applause.

I couldn't believe it; she wasn't even my woman. I mean, I had never asked her to be my woman, let alone my fiance . I didn't even like this girl as a person, couldn't even imagine loving her; yet there she stood, with real tears streaming down her face, fronting. At that point, I did the only dignified thing I could think of: I simply got up and walked out, giving her a look which was filled with pity and disgust.

Needless to say, that was not the last I ever saw of Max. Two days later she showed up at my apartment while Flo was there. In fact, Flo answered the door. I had been in the living room watching TV when I heard a bunch of loud question asking: "Are you, his lover?" Flo asked. "He's my fucken man! Who the hell are you?" Maxine replied. My mind was racing a million miles an hour in a million different directions.

I ran out into the living room. "What the fuck are you doing Maxine?!" I shouted angrily. "Nah, What the fuck are you doing? You fucking this lady?" "Bitch, if you don't get yo crazy ass away from my door...." I demanded. Maxine continued with a bunch of cussing and ranting like an obsessed stalker.

I sprinted to the door, grabbed a bunch of her blouse in my hand and hurried her across the street. "Yo, have you lost your fucken mind? What the fuck is wrong with you?" I yelled. "Who is that Bitch?" she countered, followed by a hard straight jab to my forehead! Stunned and disorientated, I slung Maxine to the ground by the blouse I still held. "Get yo crazy ass away from my place before I call the police on yo ass. "Raheem!" she whimpered. "I'm sorry, I'm sorry. Wait a minute. Let's talk Baby, let's talk!" she cried as I walked back across the street into my apartment.

Flo was standing there as I walked into the apartment with this devastated, disgusted and disappointed look on her face. "You didn't protect me," she said with tears welling. "You didn't protect me. How could you let this woman come to your house and confront me with that bullshit?" she spat with

175

increasing anger. "How could you do that to me?" she continued while gathering her things. I could not find adequate words to express my sorrow and regret. "Flo," I stammered as she hurried out of the door. I felt like shit, and I didn't know if I could ever face Flo again.

CHAPTER 23

One good deed deserves another

My building was nearly totally renovated. I'd gone to several unemployment offices and hired out-of-work electricians and plumbers. I'd hired my sister's ex-husband, a carpenter, to restore the building as soon as I bought it: all at a reasonable fee. Breakfast, lunch, and beer daily were on me. Aside from laying the tile and painting the apartments, all that needed to be done was to interview possible tenants.

I wanted only Section 8 tenants. Not only because I was guaranteed my monthly loot by the government, but also because the apartments were extremely nice and the building itself was in a desired area of Passaic, complete with schools, bus stops and major supermarkets.

I wanted to try and make life a little easier for the low-income people who found it hard to find places to live where they could get a decent night's sleep, without listening to some young hoodlums' too-loud music outside their windows all night. Where they could rest assured that the landlord would satisfy any complaints, and where the Super would keep the building clean and secure. A place their children could play in a park, without having to dodge beer and wine bottles and drug dealers. Most importantly, a place that wouldn't reflect low income. I guess I wanted to spare people the shame and embarrassment I'd gone through growing up.

In fact, after putting an ad in the local paper, I called Miss Stano at Eva's Kitchen, a homeless shelter, in search of a drug-free family in need of housing. "Hello Mr.," the woman announced, as she stepped in my office, flanked by her three sons. "My name is Margaret Pines. The shelter sent me here. They say you got a vacant apartment." "Yes, you've got the right place," I declared. "I'm Raheem. Have a seat, make yourself comfortable," I said, standing until she sat. "Hi, how are you doing?" I asked her sons. "That's Jamal, the oldest, he's 10, that's Marquise, he's eight, and that's Yusef, he's six. "Say hi," Margaret encouraged them. "They're a little shy, "she added. "That's okay," I said, understandingly.

"Miss Pines, I just need to ask you a few questions in regard to your situation. Some questions I'll ask will seem a bit personal; you don't have to answer the ones you don't want to, okay?" "Okay." "How long have you been homeless?" "Well, I guess, technically, about two years. I lived with my sister for a while, until I felt I was becoming a burden to her, so I left, which was about eight months ago." "How did you become homeless?" She looked down in embarrassment then replied, "My husband, well, long-time boyfriend, left me for another woman. I didn't have a job. He paid all the bills, so I had to leave from where we were staying because welfare wouldn't pay the rent. Said I had to wait till my name came up on the list for Section 8. They only gave me $436 a month; that ain't no money to live off, especially with three growing boys. I tried living in a furnished room, but those kinds of buildings are no place to try and raise kids. Drugs and prostitutes and all." "Yeah, I know," I responded. "So, I just moved in the shelter and did the best I could," she declared, on the brink of tears. "It's okay," I tried to comfort her. "Do you want something to drink, some water or soda or something?" I offered. "No, thank you." "We do," one of her boys chimed in. "Be quiet and sit there," Margaret retorted, clearly embarrassed. "Sure, you can have something to drink," I interrupted. "Is it okay Miss Pines?" "A soda apiece, okay, and get some cake, too." "Okay, Sir," Jamal answered and headed toward the door. "Take Yusef with you," Margaret interjected. "I'm sorry about that," she apologized. "That's okay. Now where were we? So, you don't have a Section 8, right?" I inquired. "No," she replied. "How long have you been on the list?" "Two years." "How old are you?" "36." She looked older. "Do you use drugs?" "No." "Do you drink?" "Well, I have a beer every now and again, but I ain't no alcoholic," she added, with a hint of irritation.

"I don't mean to anger you with these questions, Miss Pines, it's just that I'm trying to establish and maintain a certain environment for people's children such as yours to live comfortably. Also, I was thinking of.... Well, what I was thinking of, Miss Pines, is asking you to be the Superintendent of my building as a way of paying your rent, until you get your Section 8. The rent is $850 for a 3-bedroom apartment. This way you'll pay nothing out of your pocket, which will enable you to get on your feet in regard to necessities, like furniture, clothes and other things. And maybe even after a while you'll be able to put a little something away. Superintendent duties entail you putting the garbage in front of the building on garbage pickup days, sweeping and mopping the halls and stairs. And each month collect the other tenants' rent and take down any complaints. How does that sound?" I smiled. "Fine, just fine," she smiled back. "That's good." "Okay then, everything should be in working order by Monday. Do you drive?" "No, is that a problem," she asked, concerned. "No, not at all; nothing that we can't fix," I assured her, just as her sons walked in. I asked, "Well, are you ready to go look at your new place?" "Yes," she replied, nearly in tears.

When I dropped Miss Pines and her sons off back at the shelter, I felt good about what I had intended to do, but just as suddenly, I began to feel bad for her; not only because her cowardly husband had stepped off on her, leaving her completely destitute with his three sons; but I also felt that she had to rely on a system that was supposed to be there for her and any other American in that kind of position. Yet it had failed her and drove her to live in deplorable conditions with three young kids, as if she was someone who mattered a damn. And to think, the president, not too long ago, had signed a bill geared to eventually abolishing welfare altogether. Then, I wondered, what will the Margaret Pines of the world do to survive?

Margaret, her sons, my sister Jackie, and the guys from the moving company stood behind me whispering and kind of giggling as I prepared to cut the ribbon at the entrance of the building. I'm sure they had an idea, but probably didn't understand completely how big of an accomplishment this was for me. But it, along with everything else I'd achieved, was a very big deal for me. This building was mine! It belonged to me. I had worked long and hard to earn the money to purchase it; I had gotten a legal loan with my own merit to fix it up and insure it; and today, right here and now, I was about to see my first tenant move into it. No doubt: I was ecstatic!

They all cheered as I cut the ribbon and offered their congratulations. I beamed proudly, thanked them all, then proceeded to help the movers move in Margaret's things. I got home that evening about 7:30, feeling like a pot of gold.

CHAPTER 24

Everything that glitters ain't gold

Things had been going absolutely fantastic and I needed to celebrate. I took a long, hot bath to kind of calm myself, and shaved my head, before laying out an almond and beige sports jacket with a pair of silk, coffee-colored slacks, brown croc loafers, and a light beige, pullover crew neck shirt. I accentuated my attire with my newly purchased Rolex watch, thick gold link bracelet and chain; a monogrammed 24 karat gold ring; a 1-carat diamond cluster ring and a sleek new pair of Gucci gold frames. After applying a modest amount of a mixture of sandalwood and musk oil over my chiseled body, I got dressed, looked in the full-length mirror on the back of my bedroom door, and thought aloud "You's a handsome, sexy, Black muthafucka!" I chuckled all the way to the car, amused by myself. I mean, that night I felt strong, like somebody; and with the exception of being high, I had never felt that way before, like I mattered. I felt the surge of purpose, and I eagerly looked forward to every new day, welcoming whatever changes that the new day had up its sleeve for me. I felt absolutely "pussy good!" as my Mama used to say when she was extremely intoxicated.

"Good evening," the smiling host greeted me, as I floated through the doors of a trendy

Black folk restaurant in New York called Natalie's. "I'm good, thank you," I replied. Raheem Akmadir, 10:00 p.m. table for one." I smiled. "Sure, right this way." Mr. Versace definitely owes me some bread, because as I walked through the restaurant to be seated, all eyes followed me as if I were a fucken runway model, and being as fly as I am, I poured it on thick.

One brother even went out of his way to compliment me on how good the jacket looked on me. I ignored him at first, thinking he may have been a homosexual trying to come on to me. He evidently sensed my thoughts too, because he went on to tell me he owned a tailoring business Uptown, which was how he had a trained eye for fine clothing. I thanked him and continued to enjoy my dinner and attention. The dinner was extremely delicious. As was the attention.

I had been going over in my mind how I would spend the rest of the evening, when I overheard three brothers at the table to my left talking. It seemed a club called Sweetwater's was the place to be that night. And from what I could hear, a singer named Joe was performing there, preforming his cut, *"Things Your Man Won't Do,"* one of my favorites. The first 100 women were supposed to be admitted for only $5, so I knew a lot of them would be there.

I needed something to take my mind off of the thoughts I had of Flo. I wanted to share my good feelings of success with her. She believed in me. And I wanted to show her that I had accomplished what she thought I could. But the feelings of shame and guilt of what I had done to her superseded that thought.

I made it to Sweetwater's that evening, just as Joe was exiting the stage. The crowd was still heated, still swaying, and still singing the words to his cut, *"What Good Is a Diamond Nobody Can See?"* "I hear he's got you on lockdown, but I've got the master key." People were definitely feeling good and having a ball, but I couldn't adjust, I couldn't get into the groove. I kind of just walked around with my glass of ginger ale, stopping periodically to watch an attractive, well-endowed sister do her thing out on the dance floor to the sound of The Fugees. Outside of that, I was completely bored. But I wasn't about to give up on my night of celebration.

I decided to go to one of those exotic dancer places I had heard so much about. I figured I'd rather be at one of those places watching a woman openly than at Sweetwater's trying to fake jacks. I expected this place to be smoky, dark, and half-empty; with drunks giving naked women their money to have them put their asses an inch away from their faces. But to my surprise it was quite the opposite. Well almost.

The place was jammed with men and women of all ages and races, extremely immaculate, with bouncers and waitresses. Women still put their asses in men's faces, only it cost a minimum of $20. There must have been at least 30 girls dancing. Some on the two stages, some on people's tables, and some even half naked on men's laps. It must have been champagne night because it seemed that champagne was all that half-naked waitresses were delivering. Tony Braxton's *"Hit the Freeway"* blared as the colored strobe lights danced on the many drooling faces, and bodies gyrated.

The lights dimmed when two very beautiful young women entered through the stage entrance door. The one woman sat Indian style on the floor in front of the other woman as they began to do their thing. The two very dark-skinned women wore bright orange and blue thong bikinis, both women were well-endowed and seemed to truly enjoy showing off their wares as they simultaneously rid themselves of their tops.

The tallest of the women stood and leaned against the chrome pole, which was directly in the middle of the stage, and circled it a few times. She then stood basically at attention, back flat against the pole, reached above her head, taking hold of the pole and lifted her legs straight up in the air and held them there for at least five seconds; before parting them widely, which obviously was the cue for the other young lady to get down on her knees and slide the bottoms off the Pole Lady. The crowd went wild with applause and yelling comments like: "Oh it's on now" and "Do your thing, Baby."

From where I was standing against the cigarette machine, and because I'm 6'3", I had a bird's eye view of everything. So, when the other women on the stage fingered and mouthed Pole Lady's box, I was in complete awe. And as if that wasn't enough, when they all had their fill of the pole, they converged upon each other in a big, lusty, wild, passionate sexy session. I mean, they were doing their thing for real for real, so much so that the women seemed oblivious to the many faces and tongues that the audience members volunteered.

I was definitely not prepared for that. I mean, I can get my freak on as well as the next man, but I was truly not ready for this. This went on for nearly 30 minutes and amidst the howls, catcalls, comments, and applause, there was enough moaning and groaning to woo a monk into submission.

After the ladies exited the stage, the owner or host, or whatever he was, came onto the stage and suffered some verbal abuse for a while until he was able to calm the crowd with the offer of champagne. The man informed the crowd that the ladies would be resuming their normal routine shortly, then reminded the crowd to show their appreciation for the women by the denomination of the bills they put in the women's garters.

As the ladies came back out onto the stage and out into the crowd, I, along with plenty of other people, noticed a young lady I hadn't seen earlier. Her name was Juicy. Her full, thick, Amazonian body began seducing the crowd slowly, swaying softly to the sounds of Prince's *"I Like You."* Her brownish-blonde hair partly covered her face, and her light-green eyes scanned the crowd as she slowly turned, displaying the biggest, most well-shaped ass I had ever seen on a woman so light-skinned.

On her knees, with her back to the crowd, she reached between her legs and unsnapped the one button that held her sheer black panties together, which revealed what had to be the most gorgeous, soft-looking, biggest, heart-shaped ass in the world. Now, I try to contain myself at all costs when it comes to publicly displaying my sexual attractions for a woman, but I had to admit the sight of this sister had me out of control for a minute. My mouth lay wide open, my eyes squinted in awe, and I actually caught myself caressing the full erection in my pants. This woman was absolutely unbelievable.

But embarrassed and ashamed of allowing myself to be so moved, I quickly gathered myself together and headed for the restroom. Not surprisingly, I was the only person in the restroom, and I did have a fleeting notion to masturbate, but I just washed my hands and face, then returned to the madness.

I decided to have a seat at the bar and have a ginger ale, in an attempt to take my mind off the young lady; but as I made my way through the crowd, a short Hispanic man, overwhelmed with excitement, yanked my sleeve. "Hey man, check this out. What she does with her muscles. Check it out man," he urged.

Juicy was still on her knees, her chest lay flat on the floor and her arms stretched out from her sides. Her back was arched in such a way that from where the audience stood, her box was all there was to see: asshole completely out of view. That, to me, was amazing, considering how close the two are together. The muscles in this Juicy's vagina were obviously so strong that she opened wide and closed her box to the rhythm of the music. I mean, I've seen and felt women control their vaginal muscles before, and I have to say that I thought that was pretty amazing. But what this woman was doing with her muscles was absolutely unbelievable. It was almost as if an invisible penis was going in and out of Juicy; and the crowd was able to see how wide and deep it went into her by the way she opened up. Absolutely amazing.

As she performed this feat, she looked over her shoulder at the audience with a lustful expression on her face. Feeling myself about to fall apart again, I decided to go get that ginger ale quick. But, before I could take a step, Juicy's eyes met mine, and for a couple of seconds it seemed she was distracted from her antics, but just as quickly, she resumed, and I got that ginger ale. I drank three ginger ales straight down, one after the other, before engaging in a little banter with the two Wall Street-type guys sitting near to me. We talked about how many beautiful women that were there, and how amazing they thought it was that this had been my first time at a club like that. I assumed that it would not be my last. And after a few more ginger ales, I headed for the restroom again.

While I was in the restroom, I checked my watch and saw that it was 4:15 a.m. so I decided to have one more ginger ale and then be on my way. I'd had a hell of an evening; one I was sure I wouldn't soon forget. As I approached the bar, I noted that the Wall Street guys were talking to a woman who was sitting in my seat. I figured they were trying to buy themselves some of what the ladies had been displaying all night.

I didn't want to disturb their groove, so I walked down to the other end of the bar to place my order. I kind of squeezed my way into the crowd at the bar with my arms extended; waving a $20 bill, trying to get the barmaid's attention, when I felt something soft pressed against my back. Experience and intuition said "titties," but the fact that I was in New York made me question that. I turned around quickly, face frowned with confusion, and I found myself face to face with the one and only, very, very, sexy Juicy.

"You didn't want your seat back?" she said, sounding irritated. Surprised, overwhelmed, and delighted, but in control, I responded, "A seat is a seat." "But now you don't have one." She smiled. "It ain't important." I smiled. She gave me that look. The one that said "You ain't all that," then spun on her heels to walk away; but in mid-step, I grabbed her hand. "Hold up, Baby, let me get this drink. Do you want something?" I asked, half embarrassed for trying to play "stuff." "Moet, she smiled, obviously satisfied with the results of calling my bluff.

We found a table in the VIP section of the club. "How did you like my show?" she asked, proudly. "It was aight," trying to sound unimpressed. "You need to stop," she giggled. I couldn't help but chime in with chuckles of my own. "What's your name, Mr. Cool?" "I'm Raheem, what's yours?" I inquired. "Juicy," she retorted. "I mean, your real name." She chuckled, "That's my real name." "Yeah, aight, Miss Juicy." I laughed. "What, are you married?" she interrupted. "No, why, are you?" I asked. "No, but if you are I'd appreciate if you told me because I'd hate to be seen consorting with a married man," she said. "What makes you think I'm married?" I inquired. "Because you look married," she said flatly. "Well, I'm not." She looked at me for a long while in silence, as if trying to read my thoughts. "So, how long have you been dancing?" I asked, breaking the silence." "For about two years," she declared. "

"Is that right?" I said. "Well, aren't you going to ask why?" she questioned. "Why what?" I asked. "Aren't you going to ask why I dance, everybody else does." "Nah Baby, I ain't going to ask why. I figured you do what you do 'cause you want to do it. But I will say that you'd be a supermodel by now if you would have started modeling two years ago." I complimented. "Nope, I tried that," she retorted, butt's too big." "Oh, I didn't notice." We both laughed.

Juicy and I conversed and laughed for nearly an hour until finally I said, "Well Juice, it was definitely a pleasure meeting you. I've enjoyed your company, but it's late now, so I'm about to step. I think I'm going to stop and have some breakfast before I go home though, you want to hang out?" I offered. "Wait a minute brother, you got me mixed up. I know you don't think I'm a prostitute!" she said, with her face all frowned up. "Just cuz I can dance don't mean that I go around selling pussy. You got some mothafucken...." "Hold up, hold up Baby," I interrupted, irritated. "I didn't say you were a prostitute, or anything else. I only asked if you wanted to join me for breakfast. Besides, there are two things I don't pay for: pussy and water, and I don't intend to. You've obviously got ME mixed up with somebody else." "Listen," I said, and continued in submission, "like I said, it was a pleasure." I turned to walk away, but in mid-step Juice grabbed my hand. "Wait," but smiling a childish smile, "Let me go get my bag."

We had a large breakfast in a suite at the Milford Plaza Hotel, and as we sat there in only our drawers, we talked nearly all morning. Rochelle, Juice's real name, and I had a lot in common. She was a very intelligent and resilient young lady. Growing up in Brooklyn, the only girl and youngest of five children, she often caught hell. Her mother was a prostitute. Rochelle was born a product of her mother's dope-addicted lifestyle; which is why prostitution was a profession she now despised, and the reason why she snapped out on me at the club. Her father was obviously a white man. Along with the children in Rochelle's community, her brothers also teased, isolated, and abused her regularly. Although Rochelle hated what her mother did for a living, she nonetheless loved her mother dearly.

Rochelle even confided in me that when she was about 14 a john tried to rob her mother of her nightly earnings, including the money he had just paid her for sex. Rochelle's mother tried to fight the man off, but he was too big and strong and all she could do was cry for help. Awakened by her mother's screams, Rochelle rushed into the bedroom and saw the man choking her Mom. Rochelle said she panicked, grabbed a large kitchen knife and stabbed the man repeatedly. When I asked her what happened to the guy, she quickly changed the subject; after adding that her Mom had since stopped using drugs and had married.

Rochelle had left home at 16 to pursue a modeling career. Everybody in her neighborhood told her that she would make supermodel in no time, but all she found was casting couches and empty promises. However, she said, but she got plenty of other offers to pose nude for magazines and for parts in porn movies. She said at that time it seemed too much like prostitution.

So, to support herself she shoplifted. As a result, she went back and forth to youth correctional facilities and jails until the age of 20. What turned her life around, she reported, was when she was caught shoplifting at a mall and shared a cell in Central Booking with a dancer who had been caught in a raid at an illegal club. The dancer told her that she could make a lot of money dancing. "Men and women would pay good money just to look at you," the dancer had exclaimed. "You better go get it now, before you get too old, and all that ass starts to sag."

Rochelle said she dismissed the suggestion initially, until one day she walked into an exotic club just to see how the other girls looked and danced. That's when she decided she looked, and probably could dance better than the rest of the girls in the club. She approached the manager and had been dancing ever since. But she reasoned, she realized that her sense of rhythm wasn't exactly up to par, due to her white heritage, so she said she took dancing lessons to up her game.

She claimed to have a trendy apartment in the Village. I was impressed that at 26 years young she was doing pretty good for herself. I asked her how she was able to work her vaginal muscles the way she did. She said that when she was younger, she hated what men did so much that she pledged nothing would ever enter her box; and as a result, literally walked around with her vaginal muscles clenched all day, every day. Which is what she still did daily by force of habit.

By 8:00 a.m. we were wrestling, laughing, and playing like two kids. I had become more attracted to Juice than I had to any other woman besides Flo. Her strength, tenacity, courage, and sensitivity were overwhelming; so much so, that I held her in my arms and stroked her hair as she confided in me her deepest secrets. I truly enjoyed her company.

Surprisingly, sex was now the furthest thing from my mind.... until she kissed me. Her thick, full, moist, tender lips covered mine; she eased her soft, thick, hot tongue into my mouth. Flashes of her on stage raced through my mind, and I wanted to sex her hard and thrust myself deep inside her and bask in her screams of intense pleasure. But the more I looked into her eyes and caressed her warm voluptuous body, the more I submitted to savoring her slowly, tenderly, and passionately; only roughly when her body demanded it. I wanted to make love to Juice, to Rochelle. And to the best of my ability that's exactly what I did.

The experience with Rochelle was by far the most liberating and pleasurable experience I'd had with anyone since my release from prison, and I truly looked forward to our next encounter. "Those pussy muscles can get a Nigga strung out like a Long Island Duck!" I laughed to myself. I actually did not want it to end. I gave her my pager, home and business numbers hoping she'd call soon.

I replayed that whole morning and evening with Juice in my head during the drive home, and I concluded that I could honestly see myself in a meaningful relationship with her. However, the fact that she was an exotic dancer played heavy on my mind, and I wasn't sure how I would eventually deal with it, but I was willing to give it everything I had.

"Exclusive, Raheem speaking," I answered the phone receiver. The caller inquired about one of my apartments, but unfortunately for her there were no vacancies. All the apartments had been rented out the same week the building was restored. "I'm sorry, I can't be of help to you, but if you'd like, I'll take your name and put you on a waiting list, in the event something should become available," I offered. Clearly disappointed, the caller declined. "Okay, sorry again, bye."

Just as soon as I put the receiver in its cradle the phone rang again, "Exclusive, may I help you?" The phone had been ringing off the hook all day. Tiana and Sherry, my Exclusive Clothing employees, needed to deliver three women's dresses, one suit, and six blouses to the person on the phone before 5:00. Margaret called to inform me that the intercom at the building wasn't working properly; so, I needed to send an electrician over immediately, because Mrs. Stevens on the 3rd floor was complaining about having to walk up and down the stairs to let her children in the building. I guess it never dawned on her to give them the keys. Next, Abdul called, (one of my Guy Friday employees), needing help with the Hoffman and Kline job; so, I had to go out to help him, because everyone else was out, and it was too late in the day to hire a temp. All their offices were closed. Even Jose, my New York Clothing connection, called to inform me that I had until 9:00 p.m. to pick up the last three dozen new sports coats he'd been holding for me since Thursday, or he'd sell them. I was being pulled from all angles and I was absolutely stressed out.

The telephone rang again, I snatched it from its cradle and practically yelled "Exclusive, may I ffff.... help you?" in frustration. "Damn, Mandingo you alright?" Juicy's soft, sexy voice asked, which instantly brought a smile to my face. "Yeah, Sexy, I'm cool, just working too hard that's all," I admitted. "Well, I hope you saving some strength to play with me tonight," she chuckled. "Tonight? Don't you have to work tonight," I inquired. "No, but you sound like you got other things you'd rather do," she teased. "Nah, Baby, you know better than that. It's just that I got sooo much fucken work to do, I don't think I'll be able to get away," I explained. "That's okay, Boo, I'll come to you," she giggled. "What, are you going to get a ride from someone or catch a cab? Girl, you know how much a cab costs?" I asked. "Are you trying to talk me out of coming or what? If you don't want to see me, just say that brother, you ain't got to beat around the fucken bush," Juicy retorted, clearly irritated. "Calm down Sexy, damn, I'm just trying to make sure you'll be alright," I reasoned. "Listen, I should be done by 11:00-11:30." "So, what if I came all the way by your house and you aren't home yet?" she questioned. All right, I tell you what: tell the cab driver to drop you off at a bar called T&I's. It's on Main Avenue in Passaic, and I'll pick you up there," I instructed. "Okay, what time?" she double-checked. "11:30 maybe

12:00." "See you then, Boo," she giggled, making a kissing sound, and hung up.

I sincerely enjoyed being with Juice. We saw each other at least twice a week, but, actually, today I could have used a rest. I'd been working so much I was beginning to think I had bitten off more than I could chew. The clothing business had become a phenomenon. I had clients even as far as Delaware, Philly and Bernardsville, New Jersey. I was on the road at least four hours a day, and the cleaning/home improvement business had gotten so popular that I had to hire two more full-time workers/cleaners and buy an additional van. I was truly happy to be blessed with the amount of success I was having, but some days were more grueling than others.

Juice and I had gotten pretty close during the past three weeks, along with hours of just extraordinary sex, we also talked, and laughed a lot, about any and everything even about ourselves. We became trusting friends as well. The only thing that annoyed me with Juice was she was always full of energy. Always so perky and full of life, insatiable when it came to sex.

I was beginning to think I was getting old. She claimed that since she worked till the early morning hours, she usually slept all day, which gave her energy at night. She went to work at 10:00 p.m., and worked till 5:00 a.m. She got home at 6:00-6:30 a.m. and, I figured, slept till noon. Shit, six hours of sleep is long enough sleep for anybody. Even though most of my days were filled, I often wondered what it would be like to hang out during the daytime with Juice. I had even brought it up to her one day. She said her schedule would not allow it. I didn't pry. I didn't want her to think I was insecure or anything. But I did comment on how nice it would be to go to parks, shopping, museums, or even have dinner with her sometimes. She assured me that when she had enough money saved up, she would be able to work fewer nights and be able to spend more days with me. Quite frankly, my days were filled to the hilt, and I probably wouldn't have time to do all those things. I just wanted to see what she would say.

I arrived at T&I's at 12:30 a.m. and although I was tired as hell, the thought of seeing Juice put a little pep in my step. L. L. Cool J's *"Luv You Better"* was booming, and the crowd standing in front of the bar bobbing their heads to it and engaging in banter as the DJ mixed it up. I gave a few people the peace sign, then went inside to get my Boo.

The place was packed, and everyone was as clean as the Board of Health. I made my way through the crowd and spotted Juice standing at the end of the bar looking like brand-new money, wearing a pink silk halter and sandals. As I listened to the guy talking to her, I grinned like a Cheshire Cat. I guess he was trying to put his Mack down. She was clearly disinterested, shuffling around from side to side and looking around like a cornered mouse. "Hey, Sexy," I whispered in her ear, as I slid up behind her, wrapping my arms around her small waist as I eased closer behind her.

"Raheem!" she said excitedly, as she turned around to hug me. "Aren't you going to introduce me to your friend?" I asked holding in my laughter. "That isn't my friend," she said, irritated. "Let's go," she said, leading me to the door by the hand. Juice was truly a very beautiful, sexy, young woman.

As we walked through the bar to exit the door, it seemed that all eyes were on her. I mean, all the attention may have been on her because of the fact that she was a new face. But I'd bet my last dollar that it had more to do with the way her ass bounced with every step in those loose silk pants; her long legs; not to mention the way that warm smile seemed to be fixed on her face.

"What took you so long man? That guy's breath was boom banging," she reported as we walked out of the bar. I laughed lightly and caressed the softness of her ass as we walked to my car. As soon as we entered my house, it was on. I turned on the light and pushed her against the wall, kissing her passionately, while my hands explored her soft, sexy body. I could practically feel the wetness between her legs, as I sucked her sweet tongue.

"Wait a minute Boo," she interrupted, "I got to use the bathroom," she announced. "No, hold up Baby, let me at least get the edge off first, Baby," I replied, and continued to kiss her. "Raheem," she whined, I got to go. I got to go." "Alright, I, surrendered, and released my hold on her. She grabbed her bag and stumbled to the bathroom.

A little annoyed, I used the time she was in the bathroom to get undressed and fix us some drinks. I put Mary J Blige on the disc player and laid across the bed, waiting. My manhood began throbbing with anticipation, as thoughts of a naked Juicy ran through my mind: her long luxurious legs, her soft cream-colored skin, her perfect ass, her perky full breasts, and her thick-and-always-wet lips. Damn she was beautiful. I grew tired of waiting; she'd been in there for 20 minutes, I thought.

I figured I'd playfully scare her: so, I tiptoed to the bathroom door and pushed it open, just a little bit so that I could see her. I mean, I didn't want her to be possibly injured when I scared her. I couldn't see her at first, but I could see smoke coming from behind the door.

That caused a little concern, because as far as I knew, Juice didn't smoke. So, instead of looking through the opening of the door, I looked through the other side of the door where the hinges were. And there I saw Juice, holding one end of a thin glass tube to her mouth, with one hand holding a cigarette lighter in the other hand. My heart seemed to explode.

"Damn," I thought, "this Bitch is a crackhead." That immediately explained a lot of things like all the energy she had. It also immediately broke my heart, because I knew this would be the last time I would spend with Juice.

I must admit too, I also imagined the rush I would feel from exhaling the thick sweet crack smoke from my lungs. That scared the hell out of me because I knew what would come next. Jails, institutions, or death. Certainly, destitution and dereliction. I didn't want that shit around me. I knew how weak I used to be for drugs, and I wasn't about to tempt fate. Completely blown away by what I had just seen, I eased the door closed, went back to my bedroom and got dressed.

"What's the matter Baby, why you still got on your clothes?" Juice was smiling, still looking like God's greatest gift to man. I just looked at her, and for a moment, I was trying to find the words that I wanted to use to express my concerns for her: my fear, anger, and disappointment. But all that came out was, "Why you smoking that shit, Baby?" With a bit of surprise in her eyes, "What, you spying on me now?" she asked defensively. But, before I could answer she added, "Nah, I only smoke once in a while, you know, cuz I be tired a lot and it helps me to stay up, and work, and do things with you," she grinned and reached to undo my pants. I gently pushed her hands away. "Get your stuff together, Baby, I'm going to take you home."

"Home???" she spat. "Yeah, Sexy. I can't have that kind of shit around me." "Raheem, you're blowing this whole thing out of proportion, man. I told you I only smoke a little bit every now and then, and it's all gone," she tried to reason. "Sweetheart, just get your shit together." "So, you mean it's over with us because of a little bullshit like this?" I just looked at her in disbelief and disappointment while collecting her shoes and overnight bag from the floor and handing them to her. "Let's go!"

"I can't fucken believe this!" she yelled, as she snatched her belongings out of my hand. "I can't fucken believe you are doing this shit to me!" she said over and over again, as tears flowed down her beautiful face. "You fucken disappoint me like every fucken body else that I ever cared about or trusted."

Actually, I felt the tears well up in my own eyes too, because I felt sorry for her. Sorry for the violent ride that shit was going to take her through; sorry that she obviously didn't realize her real potential; and I was sorry for me; that I would have to X such a phenomenal person out of my life. I was devastated.

The ride back to New York was a silent one, and I barely looked at Juice except when I asked her to remember all the horror stories I had told her about my life and how it took away a very significant part of me. I warned her to ask herself if she was mentally and physically equipped to endure such drama: because "Believe me Juice. Shit get chaotic. And it is sudden and certain." She was silent.

On the way home from dropping Juice off, my mind was going a thousand miles an hour and in a thousand different directions. I dug juice. She was the kind of woman I felt I could possibly have a long-lasting relationship with. She was straight-up, funny, sexy, sweet and seemingly ambitious. She appeared to be caring, and a team player, which was everything I liked in a woman. Of course there was the loyalty, respect, and trust factor that I didn't get a chance to see. But I liked her. The only drawbacks were that she was way younger than me, an exotic dancer, and she smoked crack... I laughed, a sad laugh.

Then, suddenly, I got the overwhelming, unrelenting urge to smoke some crack myself.

CHAPTER 25

"Your life will always move in the direction of your strongest thoughts."

The aroma of that sweet smelling crack smoke haunted me from the first whiff. As soon as I got back into the house I went straight into the bathroom with hopes of another whiff. I walked in the kitchen and got a very cold bottle of water from the refrigerator, thinking that it may calm the urge. It did not work. I looked at the phone contemplating if I should call Flo. I knew that even though she was angry with me, she still would talk to me and help me through the feeling of wanting to use. However, I was ashamed of having these thoughts and even more ashamed to ask her for help after I had wronged her in the way that I did.

Actually, there were several people I could have called. I had collected many numbers during the N.A. meetings I attended. But I did not call. Instead, I wallowed in the feeling and thoughts. I could barely sleep. I wanted to use. This had become a pattern.

Every time I experienced feelings I did not want to feel, or thoughts I did not want to have, or memories I could not shake; or found myself in stressful, overwhelming situations; I would want to use drugs to numb my emotions. This had been the story of my life. I had medicated my feelings for so long that I did not know how to manage them on my own.

Whenever I thought about the nasty things Broom Hilda did to me, I would search for my friends to drink beer and smoke weed. On parent teacher night when all the parents showed up to view their kids' report cards and hear about the progress of their child and my parents did not show up, I'd leave the school and find someone to go half with me on a joint to smoke in order to numb my pain. When I thought about my Dad's absence and wondered why he did not love me, I would drink. As I got older and these same thoughts filled my head, I would use. When things did not go my way, I used. When people did not meet my unrealistic expectations, frustrated me, or abandoned me, I wanted to use. When I was angry, sad, ashamed or experiencing feelings of guilt, I always wanted to use. It was the only way I knew to relieve or numb my emotions.

When I went into work the next day, I replayed the moment that I approached the bathroom where Juice was and smelled the smoke that lingered in the air. I fantasized about exhaling the sweet smoke.

Every day for several days after work I would take the long route home, through the hood and around the areas where I knew the drug dealers hung out.

When I sold my wares to people in "the life," I would be hoping they would make me an offer that would include drugs for payment.

I thought about that shit all day. My mind was all over the place. I wanted to scream.

Finally, on my way to work one morning, I drove up Monroe Street and I saw Victor being poked in the face by an obviously irate drug dealer. I hadn't seen this dude since that night I fucked up BigHead. It appeared Victor had fucked up the dealer's package and was given the opportunity to work it off by selling the dealer's drugs going forward without pay. The dealer mushed Victor in the face so hard that Victor fell to the ground as the dealer walked away.

I got out of the car and walked over to Victor as he lay on the ground caressing a huge bump on the back of his head. As I stood over him, I spat, venomously: "Yeah, muthafucka, that fuck shit you be doing done caught up with you, huh?" Victor looked up at me from the ground with a hint of fear, coupled with a lot of pain from the bump on his head. He managed to muster a disingenuous: "Hey Raheem, how you doing bro?" he said through a forced smile.

"I don't want to hear that shit Nigga. Gimme my shit!" I demanded as I rummaged through his pockets. "Yo, yo. I ain't got nothing on me, man. I'm rocken Ali's shit. I got it stashed at my house," he whined. "Yo, my bad Rah." He continued: "You had nodded out, and I was going through it. You know how it is, man. I was gonna give you everything back when I got myself together. I was looking for you after that for a long time to pay you back, but I couldn't find you," he lied, sincerely.

"Get the fuck outta here with that bullshit," I said, annoyed, as I grabbed him by the back of his collar, pulling him up off the ground. "You gonna give me my shit right now, Nigga. Let's go."

"I told you," he protested. "All I got is Ali's product. I gotta sell some to get you your bread. Give me about an hour, and I got you." "Fuck that." I replied and pushed him toward my car. "You gone give me my shit now. I'ma take yo ass home and you gone give me what you owe me, in product." "Ah man!" he sighed.

I drove Victor to an apartment he shared with his three cousins and sister on President Street. They lived on the 1st floor, in the front of the 3-story brick building. I got out of the car with him and walked him to the apartment door. "Aight, Nigga," I warned. "In and out."

I had parked right in front of the building and could see the apartment door from my car. As I sat in the car, I began to think about what I was doing. "Raheem, you are fucken unhinged... What are you doing, man!?" I thought.

Just the day before, I'd had a phone consultation with a therapist who suggested that I set up an in-person session with him. I had expressed my concerns about not ever being able to manage some of the feelings I experienced. I told Mr. Jennings that I often experienced anger, sadness, and fear, which caused me to react irrationally.

I talked about the horrific rape experience with Broom Hilda and how I could not shake her degrading words and her prophecy of my life, and how I sometimes believed it to be true. I told him how I believed that experienced had warped my perception of sex, and women in general.

I told him how the women in my life had always appeared to let me down, disappoint me, and never met my expectations. How they appeared to be liars, manipulators and were moved by dick in any direction the dick dictated.

I talked about the relationship I had with Flo and how I felt she may have restored my faith in women/people; yet how I had hurt her; and was, ironically, the one who proved to be untrustworthy and disloyal.

I told him about my battles with drug use and how it had always been my refuge from reality. How I used it to comfort me in times of uncertainty, confusion, and fear.

Mr. Jennings inquired about my accomplishments and aspirations. I admitted that I felt a sense of accomplishment for building my businesses but sometimes accredited a huge part of the success to manipulation, deceit, and my "big funky dick" (as Broom Hilda called it). I confided that I wanted to go back to school and get certifications and degrees in Substance Abuse or Social Work but feared that I was not smart enough. Perhaps, subconsciously, I believed that Broom Hilda was right about me being dumb.

I told Mr. Jennings about my son and daughter. How I wanted to be the light of their lives and how important it was for me to be the example to my son of what a man is supposed to be. He is to be self-sufficient, humble, responsible and strong. I told him that I wanted to teach my daughter how to be a lady and what to expect from a man; as well as what kind of behavior she should and should not accept from a man. I wanted to show them that the world is enormous and not to be afraid to explore it: to go after their dreams and live life abundantly. I told Mr. Jennings that I wanted my children to have almost everything.

My thoughts were interrupted by Victor handing me a bundle of dope and seven dimes of crack through the driver side window. "This all I can stand right now, Rah. But I got you. Come back later tonight and I'll have the rest of what I owe, Aight?" "Yeah, aight Nigga. I don't wanna have to chase you down," I retorted. "Nah, like I said before, my bad. Won't happen again," Victor assured. "Aight," I said, as I pulled off.

My palms were sweating so bad that I had to put the drugs in my pocket so that they would not be soaked with sweat. My stomach rumbled and I fantasized about the euphoric feeling of the dope flowing through my body, followed by the extreme, dick-hardening rush of the crack when I exhaled the smoke.

Just as suddenly, I imagined the familiar disappointment in my Momma's face when she realizes that I am getting high; the gradual loss of everything I managed to build. Businesses, buildings, cars, clothes, jewelry, and dignity would all be a sad memory if I took a hit of either.

I parked the car and walked to my apartment, lost in my thoughts. As soon as I closed the door behind me, I reached in my pocket and began to toy with the drugs in my hand. I walked into the kitchen, sat at the table and placed the drugs on the table in front of me.

My mind was going a thousand miles an hour in a thousand different directions. I knew in that moment I had the opportunity to call someone to talk me through the feeling that would lead me to ruin my life; to help me avoid the horrible ordeal of being dragged by the face to a drug-addicted, dirty mess.

Or, I rationalized, this time, maybe, I could use these drugs... just this one time; and then go back to my normal living. That maybe, this time, I will find the strength that I had never had before to just walk away after this one last time. Maybe...

Connect with Raheem on social media

TikTok
https://www.tiktok.com/@almosteverything630

Instagram
https://www.instagram.com/almosteverything630

Facebook
https://www.facebook.com/raheem.akmadir

LinkedIn
https://www.linkedin.com/in/raheem-akmadir

Twitter
https://www.twitter.com/aeverything630

YouTube
https://www.youtube.com/@raheemnahsif7969

Made in the USA
Monee, IL
08 January 2025

76106136R00125